eBook and Digital Learning Tools for

A Progressive Era for Whom?

African Americans in an Age of Reform, 1890-1920

MICHELLE KUHL

Carefully scratch off the silver coating with a coin to see your personal redemption code.

This code can be used only once and cannot be shared!

If the code has been scratched off when you receive it, the code may not be valid. Once the code has been scratched off, this access card cannot be returned to the publisher. You may buy access at **www.oup.com/us/debatingamericanhistory**.

The code on this card is valid for 2 years from the date of first purchase. Complete terms and conditions are available at **https://oup-arc.com.**

Access length: 6 months from redemption of the code.

VIA THE OUP SITE

Visit **www.oup.com/us/debatingamericanhistory**

Select the edition you are using and the student resources for that edition.

Click the link to upgrade your access to the student resources.

Follow the on-screen instructions.

Enter your personal redemption code when prompted on the checkout screen.

VIA YOUR SCHOOL'S LEARNING MANAGEMENT SYSTEM

Log in to your instructor's course.

When you click a link to a protected resource, you will be prompted to register for access.

Follow the on-screen instructions.

Enter your personal redemption code when prompted on the checkout screen.

For assistance with code redemption or registration, please contact customer support at **arc.support@oup.com**.

PRAISE FOR DEBATING AMERICAN HISTORY

"Debating American History repositions the discipline of history as one that is rooted in discovery, investigation, and interpretation."

—Ingrid Dineen-Wimberly, University of California, Santa Barbara

"Debating American History is an excellent replacement for a 'big assignment' in a course. It offers a way to add discussion to a class, and it is a perfect 'active learning' assignment, in a convenient package."

—Gene Rhea Tucker, Temple College

"The advantage that Debating American History has over other projects and texts currently available is that this brings a very clear and focused organization to the notion of classroom debate. The terms of the debate are clear. The books introduce students to historiography and primary sources. Most of all, the project re-envisions the way that US history should be taught. No other textbook or set of teaching materials does what these books do when taken together as the sum of their parts."

—Ian Hartman, University of Alaska

DEBATING AMERICAN HISTORY

A PROGRESSIVE ERA FOR WHOM?

DEBATING AMERICAN HISTORY

Series Editors: Joel M. Sipress, David J. Voelker

Conflict and Accommodation in Colonial New Mexico
Jonathan Decoster

The Powhatans and the English in the Seventeenth-Century Chesapeake
David J. Voelker

Democracy and the US Constitution
Joel M. Sipress

The Causes of the Civil War
Joel M. Sipress

Emancipation and the End of Slavery
Joel M. Sipress

Industrialization and Social Conflict in the Gilded Age
Joel M. Sipress

A Progressive Era for Whom?: African Americans in an Age of Reform, 1890–1920
Michelle Kuhl

The Politics of Prosperity: Mass Consumer Culture in the 1920s
Kimberley A. Reilly

Fire in the Streets: The Social Crisis of the 1960s
Joel M. Sipress

DEBATING AMERICAN HISTORY

A PROGRESSIVE ERA FOR WHOM?

African Americans in an Age of Reform, 1890–1920

Michelle Kuhl
UNIVERSITY OF WISCONSIN OSHKOSH

NEW YORK OXFORD
OXFORD UNIVERSITY PRESS

Oxford University Press is a department of the University of Oxford. It furthers the University's objective of excellence in research, scholarship, and education by publishing worldwide. Oxford is a registered trade mark of Oxford University Press in the UK and certain other countries.

Published in the United States of America by Oxford University Press
198 Madison Avenue, New York, NY 10016, United States of America.

For titles covered by Section 112 of the US Higher Education Opportunity Act, please visit www.oup.com/us/he for the latest information about pricing and alternate formats.

Library of Congress Cataloging-in-Publication Data

Names: Kuhl, Michelle, author.
Title: A Progressive Era for whom? : African Americans in an age of reform, 1890–1920 / Michelle Kuhl, University of Wisconsin-Oshkosh.
Description: New York : Oxford University Press, [2020] | Series: Debating American history | Includes bibliographical references and index. | Summary: "A higher education History primary source textbook that embraces an argument based model for teaching history. It is part of the Debating American History series, and covers the African American experience during the Age of Reform (1890–1920)"—Provided by publisher.
Identifiers: LCCN 2020001514 (print) | LCCN 2020001515 (ebook) | ISBN 9780197519196 (paperback) | ISBN 9780197519202 (epub) | ISBN 9780197527047
Subjects: LCSH: African Americans—History—1877–1964—Sources. | African Americans—History—1877–1964—Study and teaching. | Progressivism (United States politics)—History. | Social change—United States—History—19th century. | Social change—United States—History—20th century.
Classification: LCC E185.6 .K85 2020 (print) | LCC E185.6 (ebook) | DDC 973/.049607300904—dc23
LC record available at https://lccn.loc.gov/2020001514
LC ebook record available at https://lccn.loc.gov/2020001515

Printing number: 9 8 7 6 5 4 3 2 1
Printed by LSC Communications, Inc., United States of America

TABLE OF CONTENTS

LIST OF FIGURES, TABLES, AND MAPS

Figures

Tables

Maps

ABOUT THE AUTHOR

Michelle Kuhl is an Associate Professor at the University of Wisconsin Oshkosh. Her scholarly focus is on activism against racial violence during the late nineteenth and early twentieth century. She teaches courses on African American History, US Women's History, and the History of Pirates. Since 2018 she has been the Chief Reader of the Advanced Placement US History exam. In the 1980s she earned an undergraduate history degree at North Carolina State University, and she earned a master's and PhD in US History at Binghamton University. She likes studies that say a messy desk is a sign of genius.

ACKNOWLEDGMENTS

First I thank David Voelker for his vision of this series and inviting me to join him. A big thank-you to Charles Cavaliere at Oxford University Press for embracing this project and seeing it through. Additional thanks to Danica Donovan of Oxford for her patience in my many "I need one more day" emails. The University of Wisconsin Oshkosh and the History Department supported my scholarship through the Curriculum Modification program. The bulk of the work I did was in the presence of and the kind but firm accountability and support of my Stuart Research Group: Emmet Sandberg and Margaret Hostetler. For general inspiration and friendship, I thank Carol Faulkner. Linda Janke and Peter Hennigan always uplift my spirits with frequent visits and general conviviality. My Tuesday night crew makes the rest of the work week possible, so thank you to Za Barron, Becky Bartow, Christie Demosthenous, Andrea Jacobs, Memuna Khan, Samara Hamze, Julie Schulte, Wendy Stelzer, and Courtney Van Auken. Along this journey I was happy to know Kim Reilly was running a parallel track balancing scholarship, teaching, and parenting. Solidarity. Most of all I thank my family, Jeff, Clio, and Eliza Pickron, for their patience and support. I would also like to thank the reviewers of this edition: Andrew C. Baker, Texas A&M University-Commerce; Maurice Isserman, Hamilton College; Tramaine Anderson, Tarrant County College; Ian Hartman, University of Alaska Anchorage; Michael Holm, Boston University; Matthew Tribbe, Fullerton College; Thomas W. Devine, CSU Northridge; and Robert J. Allison, Suffolk University.

SERIES INTRODUCTION

Although history instruction has grown richer and more varied over the past few decades, many college-level history teachers remain wedded to the coverage model, whose overriding design principle is to cover huge swaths of history, largely through the use of textbooks and lectures. The implied rationale supporting the coverage model is that students must be exposed to a wide array of facts, narratives, and concepts in order to have the necessary background both to be effective citizens and to study history at a more advanced level—something that few students actually undertake. Although coverage-based courses often afford the opportunity for students to encounter primary sources, the imperative to cover an expansive body of material dominates these courses, and the main assessment technique, whether implemented through objective or written exams, is to require students to identify or reproduce authorized knowledge.

Unfortunately, the coverage model has been falling short of its own goals since its very inception in the late nineteenth century. Educators and policymakers have been lamenting the historical ignorance of American youth going back to at least 1917, as Stanford professor of education Sam Wineburg documented in his illuminating exposé of the history of standardized tests of historical knowledge.[1] In 2010, the *New York Times* declared that "History is American students' worst subject," basing this judgment on yet another round of abysmal standardized test scores.[2] As we have documented in our own historical research, college professors over the past century have episodically criticized the coverage model and offered alternatives. Recently, however, college-level history instructors have been forming a scholarly community to improve the teaching of the introductory course by doing research that includes rigorous analysis of student learning. A number of historians who have become involved in this discipline-based pedagogical research, known as

1 Sam Wineburg, "Crazy for History," *Journal of American History* 90 (March 2004): 1401–1414.

2 Sam Dillon, "U.S. Students Remain Poor at History, Tests Show," *New York Times*, June 14, 2011. Accessed online at http://www.nytimes.com/2011/06/15/education/15history.html?emc=eta1&pagewanted=print.

the Scholarship of Teaching and Learning (SoTL), have begun to mount a challenge to the coverage model.[3]

Not only has the coverage model often achieved disappointing results by its own standards, it has also proven to be ineffective at helping students learn how to think historically, which has long been a stated goal of history education. As Lendol Calder argued in a seminal 2006 article, the coverage model works to "cover up" or "conceal" the nature of historical thinking.[4] The eloquent lecture or the unified textbook narrative reinforces the idea that historical knowledge consists of a relatively straightforward description of the past. Typical methods of covering content hide from students not only the process of historical research—the discovery and interpretation of sources—but also the ongoing and evolving discussions among historians about historical meaning. In short, the coverage model impedes historical thinking by obscuring the fact that history is a complex, interpretative, and argumentative discourse.

Informed by the scholarship of the processes of teaching and learning, contemporary reformers have taken direct aim at the assumption that factual and conceptual knowledge must precede more sophisticated forms of historical study. Instead, reformers stress that students must learn to think historically by doing—at a novice level—what expert historians do.[5]

With these ideas in mind, we thus propose an argument-based model for teaching the introductory history course. In the argument-based model, students participate in a contested, evidence-based discourse about the human past. In other words, students are asked to argue about history. And by arguing, students develop the dispositions and habits of mind that are central to the discipline of history.[6] As the former American Historical Association (AHA) president Kenneth Pomeranz noted in late 2013, historians should consider seeing general education history courses as valuable "not for the sake of 'general knowledge'

---

3 See Lendol Calder, "Uncoverage: Toward a Signature Pedagogy for the History Survey," *Journal of American History* 92 (March 2006): 1358–1370; Joel M. Sipress and David J. Voelker, "The End of the History Survey Course: The Rise and Fall of the Coverage Model," *Journal of American History* 97 (March 2011): 1050–1066; and Penne Restad, "American History Learned, Argued, and Agreed Upon," in *Team-Based Learning in the Social Sciences and Humanities*, ed. Michael Sweet and Larry K. Michaelson, 159–180 (Sterling, VA: Stylus, 2012). For an overview of the Scholarship of Teaching and Learning (SoTL) in history, see Joel M. Sipress and David Voelker, "From Learning History to Doing History: Beyond the Coverage Model," in *Exploring Signature Pedagogies: Approaches to Teaching Disciplinary Habits of Mind*, ed. Regan Gurung, Nancy Chick, and Aeron Haynie, 19–35 (Sterling, VA: Stylus, 2008). Note also that the International Society for the Scholarship of Teaching and Learning in History was formed in 2006. See http://www.indiana.edu/~histsotl/blog/.

4 Calder, "Uncoverage," 1362–1363.

5 For influential critiques of the "facts first" assumption, see Sam Wineburg, "Crazy for History," *Journal of American History* 90 (March 2004): 1401–1414; and Calder, "Uncoverage."

6 For discussions of argument-based courses, see Barbara E. Walvoord and John R. Breihan, "Arguing and Debating: Breihan's History Course," in Barbara E. Walvoord and Lucille P. McCarthy, *Thinking and Writing in College: A Naturalistic Study of Students in Four Disciplines* (Urbana, IL: National Council of Teachers of English, 1990), 97–143; Todd Estes, "Constructing the Syllabus: Devising a Framework for Helping Students Learn to Think Like Historians," *History Teacher* 40 (February 2007): 183–201; Joel M. Sipress, "Why Students Don't Get Evidence and What We Can Do About It," *The History Teacher* 37 (May 2004): 351–363; David J. Voelker, "Assessing Student Understanding in Introductory Courses: A Sample Strategy," *The History Teacher* 41 (August 2008): 505–518.

but for the intellectual operations you can teach."[7] Likewise, the AHA "Tuning Project" defines the discipline in a way much more consistent with an argument-based course than with the coverage model: "History is a set of evolving rules and tools that allows us to interpret the past with clarity, rigor, and an appreciation for interpretative debate. It requires evidence, sophisticated use of information, and a deliberative stance to explain change and continuity over time. As a profoundly public pursuit, history is essential to active and empathetic citizenship and requires effective communication to make the past accessible to multiple audiences. As a discipline, history entails a set of professional ethics and standards that demand peer review, citation, and toleration for the provisional nature of knowledge."[8] We have designed *Debating American History* with these values in mind.

In the coverage-based model, historical knowledge is seen as an end in itself. In the argument-based model, by contrast, the historical knowledge that students must master serves as a body of evidence to be employed in argument and debate. While the ultimate goal of the coverage approach is the development of a kind of cultural literacy, the argument-based history course seeks to develop historical modes of thinking and to encourage students to incorporate these modes of thinking into their daily lives. Particularly when housed within a broader curriculum that emphasizes engaged learning, an argument-based course prepares students to ask useful questions in the face of practical problems and challenges, whether personal, professional, or civic. Upon encountering a historical claim, such as those that frequently arise in political discussions, they will know how to ask important questions about context, evidence, and logic. In this way, the argument-based course fulfills the discipline's long-standing commitment to the cultivation of engaged and informed citizens.[9]

While there is no single correct way to structure an argument-based course, such courses do share a number of defining characteristics that drive course design.[10] In particular, argument- based courses:

1. ARE ORGANIZED AROUND SIGNIFICANT HISTORICAL QUESTIONS ABOUT WHICH HISTORIANS THEMSELVES DISAGREE.

Argument-based courses are, first and foremost, question-driven courses in which "big" historical questions (rather than simply topics or themes) provide the overall organizational structure. A "big" historical question is one about which historians themselves

7 Kenneth Pomeranz, "Advanced History for Beginners: Why We Should Bring What's Best about the Discipline into the Gen Ed Classroom," *Perspectives on History* (Nov. 2013), at http://www.historians.org/publications-and-directories/perspectives-on-history/november-2013/advanced-history-for-beginners-why-we-should-bring-what's-best-about-the-discipline-into-the-gen-ed-classroom.

8 This definition reflects the state of the Tuning Project as of September 2013. For more information, see "AHA History Tuning Project: History Discipline Core," at http://www.historians.org/teaching-and-learning/current-projects/tuning/history-discipline-core. Accessed August 3, 2014.

9 As recently as 2006, the AHA's Teaching Division reasserted the importance of history study and scholarship in the development of globally aware citizens. Patrick Manning, "Presenting History to Policy Makers: Three Position Papers," *Perspectives: The Newsmagazine of the American Historical Association* 44 (March 2006): 22–24.

10 Our approach to course design is deeply influenced by Grant Wiggins and Jay McTighe, *Understanding by Design*, 2nd ed. (Upper Saddle River, NJ: Pearson Education, 2006).

disagree and that has broad academic, intellectual, or cultural implications. Within these very broad parameters, the types of questions around which a course may be organized can vary greatly. The number of "big" questions addressed, however, must be relatively limited in number (perhaps three to five over the course of a typical fifteen-week semester), so that students can pursue the questions in depth.

2. SYSTEMATICALLY EXPOSE STUDENTS TO RIVAL POSITIONS ABOUT WHICH THEY MUST MAKE INFORMED JUDGMENTS.

Argument-based courses systematically expose students to rival positions about which they must form judgments. Through repeated exploration of rival positions on a series of big questions, students see historical debate modeled in a way that shatters any expectation that historical knowledge is clear-cut and revealed by authority. Students are thus confronted with the inescapable necessity to engage, consider, and ultimately evaluate the merits of a variety of perspectives.

3. ASK STUDENTS TO JUDGE THE RELATIVE MERITS OF RIVAL POSITIONS ON BASIS OF HISTORICAL EVIDENCE.

To participate in historical argument, students must come to see historical argument as more than a matter of mere opinion. For this to happen, students must learn to employ evidence as the basis for evaluating historical claims. Through being repeatedly asked to judge the relative merits of rival positions on the basis of evidence, students come to see the relationship between historical evidence and historical assertions.

4. REQUIRE STUDENTS TO DEVELOP THEIR OWN POSITIONS FOR WHICH THEY MUST ARGUE ON THE BASIS OF HISTORICAL EVIDENCE.

In an argument-based course, the ultimate aspiration should be for students to bring their own voices to bear on historical discourse in a way that is thoroughly grounded in evidence. Students must therefore have the opportunity to argue for their own positions. Such positions may parallel or synthesize those of the scholars with which they have engaged in the course or they may be original. In either case, though, students must practice applying disciplinary standards of evidence.

Learning to argue about history is, above all, a process that requires students to develop new skills, dispositions, and habits of mind. Students develop these attributes through the act of arguing in a supportive environment where the instructor provides guidance and feedback. The instructor is also responsible for providing students with the background, context, and in-depth materials necessary both to fully understand and appreciate each big question and to serve as the body of evidence that forms the basis for judgments and arguments. While argument-based courses eschew any attempt to provide comprehensive coverage, they ask students to think deeply about a smaller number of historical questions, and in the process of arguing about the selected questions, students will develop significant content knowledge in the areas emphasized.

While a number of textbooks and readers in American history incorporate elements of historical argumentation, there are no published materials available that are specifically designed to support an argument-based course. *Debating American History* consists of a series of modular units, each focused on a specific topic and question in American history that will support all four characteristics of an argument-based course noted earlier. Each of the modules is designed for a roughly three- to four-week course unit. Instructors will select units that support their overall course design, perhaps incorporating one or two modules into an existing course or structuring an entire course around three to five such units. (Instructors, of course, are free to supplement the modular units with other materials of their choosing, such as additional primary documents, secondary articles, multimedia materials, and book chapters.) By focusing on a limited number of topics, students will be able to engage in in-depth historical argumentation, including consideration of multiple positions and substantial bodies of evidence.

Each unit will have the following elements:

1. THE BIG QUESTION

The unit will begin with a brief narrative introduction that will pose the central question of the unit and provide general background.

2. HISTORIANS' CONVERSATIONS

This section will establish the debate by providing two or three original essays that present distinct and competing scholarly positions on the Big Question. While these essays will make occasional reference to major scholars in the field, they are not intended to provide historiographical overviews, but rather to provide models of historical argumentation through the presentation and analysis of evidence.

3. DEBATING THE QUESTION

Each module will include a variety of materials containing evidence for students to use to evaluate the various positions and develop a position of their own. Materials may include primary source documents, images, a timeline, maps, or brief secondary sources. The specific materials will vary depending upon the nature of the question. Some modules will include detailed case studies that focus on a particular facet of the Big Question.

For example, one module that we have developed for an early American history course focuses on the following Big Question: "How were the English able to displace the thriving Powhatan people from their Chesapeake homelands in the seventeenth century?" The Historians' Conversations section includes two essays: "Position #1: The Overwhelming Advantages of the English"; and "Position #2: Strategic Mistakes of the Powhatans." The unit materials allow students to undertake a guided exploration of both Powhatan and English motivations and strategies. The materials include two case studies that serve specific pedagogical purposes. The first case study asks the question, "Did Pocahontas Rescue John Smith from Execution?" Answering this question requires grappling with the nature of primary sources and weighing additional evidence from secondary sources; given historians' confidence that Powhatan did adopt Smith during his captivity, the case study also raises important questions about Powhatan strategy. The second case study focuses on the 1622 surprise attack that the Powhatans (led by Opechancanough) launched against the English, posing the question: "What was the Strategy behind the 1622 Powhatan Surprise Attack?" Students wrestle with a number of scholarly perspectives regarding Opechancanough's purpose and the effectiveness of his strategy. Overall, this unit introduces students to the use of primary sources and the process of weighing different historical interpretations. Because of Disney's 1995 film *Pocahontas*, many students begin the unit thinking that they already know about the contact between the Powhatans and the English; many of them also savor the chance to bring critical, historical thinking to bear on this subject, and doing so deepens their understanding of how American Indians responded to European colonization.

Along similar lines, the Big Question for a module on the Gilded Age asks, "Why was industrialization in the late nineteenth century accompanied by such great social and political turmoil?" The materials provided allow students to explore the labor conflicts of the period as well as the Populist revolt and to draw conclusions regarding the underlying causes of the social and political upheavals. Primary sources allow students to delve into labor conflicts from the perspectives of both the workers and management, to explore both Populist and anti-Populist perspectives. Three short case studies allow students to examine specific instances of social conflict in depth. A body of economic data from the late nineteenth century is also included.

Many history instructors, when presented with the argument-based model, find its goals to be compelling, but they fear that it is overly ambitious—that introductory-level students will be incapable of engaging in historical thinking at an acceptable level. But we must ask: how well do students learn under the coverage model? Student performance varies in an argument-based course, but it varies widely in a coverage-based course as well. In our experience, most undergraduate students are capable of achieving a basic-level competence at identifying and evaluating historical interpretations and using primary and secondary sources as evidence to make basic historical arguments. We not only have evidence of this success in the form of our own grade books, but we have studied our students' learning to document the success of our approach.[11] Students can indeed learn how to think like historians at a novice level, and in doing so they will gain both an appreciation for the discipline and develop a set of critical skills and dispositions that will contribute to their overall higher education. For this to happen, however, a course must be "backward designed" to promote and develop historical thinking. As historian Lawrence Gipson (Wabash College) asked in a 1916 AHA discussion, "Will the student catch 'historical-mindedness' from his instructor like the mumps?"[12] The answer, clearly, is "no."

In addition to the modular units focused on big questions, instructors will also be provided with a brief instructors' manual, entitled "Developing an Argument-Based Course."

11 See Sipress, "Why Students Don't Get Evidence," and Voelker, "Assessing Student Understanding."

12 Lawrence H. Gipson, "Method of the Elementary Course in the Small College," *The History Teacher's Magazine* 8 (April 1917), 128. (The conference discussion took place in 1916.)

This volume will provide instructors with guidance and advice on course development, as well as with sample in-class exercises and assessments. Additionally, each module includes an Instructor's Manual. Together, these resources will assist instructors with the process of creating an argument-based course, whether for a relatively small class at a liberal arts college or for a large class of students at a university. These resources can be used in both face-to-face and online courses.

The purpose of *Debating American History* is to provide instructors with both the resources and strategies that they will need to design such a course. This textbook alternative leaves plenty of room for instructor flexibility, and it requires instructors to carefully choose, organize, and introduce the readings to students, as well as to coach students through the process of thinking historically, even as they deepen their knowledge and understanding of particular eras and topics.

Joel M. Sipress
Professor of History
University of Wisconsin-Superior

David J. Voelker
Professor of Humanities and History
University of Wisconsin-Green Bay

DEBATING AMERICAN HISTORY

A PROGRESSIVE ERA FOR WHOM?

THE BIG QUESTION

A PROGRESSIVE ERA?

Is it racially insensitive to call the early twentieth century the Progressive Era if African Americans did not share in this progress?

To make order out of the chaos of the past, historians look for patterns and name eras. US history textbooks commonly call the early twentieth century the Progressive Era. Although there are some disagreements about when the Progressive Era ended, many historians set World War I as the next major era, and then the "Roaring Twenties." Everyone agrees to call the 1930s the "Great Depression," and similarly most historians recognize that World War II was a major event that deserves its own category.

The Progressive Era is a little trickier since it does not coincide with a war or a clearly defined set of actions or ideas. In the late nineteenth and early twentieth century, multiple people and organizations worked to identify and address substantial challenges to society. They were a loose coalition who had many differences, but historians call them "Progressives" because they shared at least three characteristics. One, Progressives believed in the possibility—and powerful necessity—of progress. Two, Progressives thought that study and scientific knowledge could help them understand and craft effective solutions to problems. And three, Progressives thought larger organizations and the government could robustly tackle problems. Since many of the problems were large and powerful, only a large and powerful entity could find and implement solutions.

However, scholars who study African American history do not follow the same pattern of naming of eras. Most textbooks focused on black history organize chapters by Slavery, Civil War, Emancipation, Reconstruction, and then the rise of Jim Crow segregation. World War I is a turning point because it jump-starts the Great Migration, which then leads into the Harlem Renaissance, and then the Great Depression and World War II.

This book asks you to examine whether the Progressive Era is the right term for the early twentieth century. Is it okay to have separate names for eras for national history and African American history? Is it wrong to discount the experiences of African Americans when naming eras? Is there a way to bridge the gap and find some common ground to include African Americans within the way we define and understand the Progressive Era?

This introductory essay will cover the context of the late nineteenth and early twentieth century and describe both the traditional way to interpret the Progressive Era as well as what challenges faced African Americans at this time. Then two essays will offer competing perspectives on this time period. The last and largest section is a collection of primary documents so that you, the student, can research and draw your own conclusion. Ultimately, you need to investigate the Big Question for this book: *Was the early twentieth century a Progressive Era for African Americans?*

THE PROBLEMS OF THE GILDED AGE

For many decades, scholars have viewed the Progressive Era as reformers solving the problems created by the Gilded Age. (Historians debate the proper dates for the Gilded Age, but the usual chronology is 1865–1900.) During the Gilded Age, clever businessmen like John D. Rockefeller and Andrew Carnegie created giant companies of railroads, steel, and coal and became millionaires. People built huge factories that employed thousands of people. Railroad lines connected the east and west coasts, enabling goods to travel the country and create more riches for corporate enterprises and a higher standard of living for many ordinary folks. The jobs created by the mushrooming of industrial capitalism drew immigrants from around the world, particularly from southern and eastern Europe. America is wealthy and powerful today, but that was not always the case. Before the Gilded Age, European countries considered America to be a backward nation of farmers with little importance in the world. During the Gilded Age, however, America became one of the wealthiest nations, with innovative technology widely admired and imitated.

However, all of this rapid development created new sorts of problems. One was the tension between labor and capital. Engineers and industrialists figured out ways to make jobs streamlined, requiring less skill. Many jobs in coal mining, steel making, and railroad construction could be done by workers with minimal training. Consequently, owners could easily replace them, and they had little of the bargaining power that artisans (carpenters, brick masons, and other craft workers) formerly had. Workers in these unskilled jobs faced dangerous working conditions, low pay, and little control over the pace of their tasks. Increasingly workers fought back in a series of massive strikes that sometimes turned violent. Some Americans sympathized with workers and their fight for better pay and conditions, while some Americans thought union organizers and strikers were dangerous radicals. All Americans were worried that there was no clear solution in sight, and that the price of industrial riches might well be ongoing class warfare.

Cities that had grown too fast were another central feature of the Gilded Age. Just walking down the sidewalk in a city like Boston or New York was, frankly, disgusting. People in rural areas had a simple way of dealing with garbage—they tossed it in the yard and let nature take care of it. If you cooked a chicken for dinner, for example, you killed the chicken, pulled out the guts, plucked the feathers, and then cooked the chicken. After eating, you tossed aside the bones and leftovers. Left in a pile in the woods a few hundred yards from the house, scavenger animals and microbes would eventually break down all those components. Human waste went into outhouses. Animal carcasses, like a beloved elder plough horse that passed away, could be dragged into the woods to decompose. But what about when this farming family moved to the city and lived in a tenement? They had no outhouse, so they eliminated waste in chamber pots and tossed them out the window into the streets. If they bought and cooked a chicken for dinner, they tossed the guts and feathers and bones into the streets. There were no plough horses, but thousands of horses in the city pulled cabs, and their refuse (up a gallon of urine a day per horse, for example) also flowed in the streets. When the cab horse died, the owner left the corpse to rot in the street.

Cities that grew quickly struggled with clean drinking water, sanitation systems, growing crime, and political corruption. The size of city governments created during the antebellum period simply was not large or sophisticated enough to deal with the magnitude of problems created by the fast-growing population.

Another concern created by the Gilded Age rise in industrial capitalism was the influx of immigrants coming to work at the expanding factories. Many Americans were quite proud that their country existed as a beacon of hope and opportunity, but other Americans expressed hostility toward what they called the "new immigrants" who came from southern and eastern Europe. Some of the native-born, Protestant Americans openly stated that these newcomers, many of whom were Catholic, Eastern Orthodox, or Jewish, would not assimilate to the existing American culture. Authors like Madison Grant argued these new immigrants were not the same racial stock as the old Americans and would dilute the country's proud Anglo Saxon heritage. Other Americans were less concerned that the immigrants would undermine white supremacy but did worry that they worked in dangerous conditions and lived in tenement slums with poor ventilation, water, and other health concerns.

One of the biggest concerns of the Gilded Age was the rise of monopolies, or trusts. Business men in the late nineteenth century found ways (not always legal) of investing their money to create related business concerns that helped their company thrive. J. D. Rockefeller, for example, bought up multiple oil companies so that he could make deals with the railroads and avoid competing with other companies. He had so much freight to move that railroad companies could not refuse his demands without losing a great deal of business. Andrew Carnegie made steel and bought companies that fed into the steel-making process. He also bought land where iron ore could be found, companies that mined the ore, factories that turned the ore into steel, and enterprises that turned the steel into various products. He therefore controlled all the stages of production and minimized costs to himself. Big businessmen became so powerful they could influence, or even dictate, the prices of their goods, overriding supply and demand. They could determine the salary and conditions of workers, and even pressure politicians to pass laws favorable to them. Americans worried that the growing power of these business monopolies undermined democracy and the ability of common people to have a fair chance to work, start a business, or make political decisions for the good of the whole. Ultimately, the many excesses of the Gilded Age thus seemed to beg for real changes to all these huge problems.

SOUTHERN CHALLENGES

The South also provided reformers looking to improve society many areas of concern. Thanks to the New South movement championed by white men like Henry Grady in Atlanta, industrial advancement occurred in some areas of the South. However, much of the former Confederacy remained extremely poor in the wake of the economic devastation of the Civil War. Local reformers and activists from outside the region thus easily identified challenges in the areas of health, education, child labor, and race relations.

Health activists who wanted to eradicate disease epidemics collected data in rural areas of the South and were shocked at what they found. In great part because of poor sanitation ("open air privies" were the norm), flies and other insects spread disease that sapped the health and strength of many southerners. At a children's health clinic in Escambia, Florida, in 1922, workers found that three-fifths of the children were underweight, one-half had never used a toothbrush, one-half had poor vision, and three-fourths had hookworm.[1] Hookworm is a parasite that thrives in unsanitary conditions. Contaminated soil contains eggs and larvae of hookworm. If you walk barefoot on such soil, the larvae can go through your skin and then mature in your intestine. The worms feed on the nutrients in your body, causing stomach pain and loss of energy. Hookworm infections can stunt the growth of children. Many towns did not have clean water supplies, midwives were not familiar with germ theory and so did not disinfect their hands or tools, and epidemics spread quickly.

Progressive reformers also targeted education. The South did not have the same emphasis on widespread education as the North. The Puritan emphasis on Bible reading left a legacy of education in New England. By contrast, the South had high levels of illiteracy and a poor infrastructure. Local districts did not want to invest much money in education for white or black children. School buildings were small and decrepit, teachers were poorly paid, and administrations provided little funding for books or supplies. Most parents wanted to keep their kids to work on the farms or in the mills, and when questioned, children stated they preferred to be with their parents rather than go to school.

Although parents and children thought it natural for children to work alongside parents, reformers were horrified at the widespread use of child labor in the South. The farm tradition of child labor translated to the new textile mills. Progressive activists thought it was perhaps fine for a child to grow up working on the fresh air of the farm (outside school hours) but were opposed to children working 12- to 14-hour days confined indoors in unhealthy textile mills.

One of the biggest challenges reformers saw in the South was an apparently generally hostile attitude toward change. Most white southerners wanted local control of their affairs—and they did not want outsiders, particularly northerners, coming to their region and telling them how backward they were. And note how little this strain of progressive reform concerned itself with issues related to race.

PROGRESSIVE SOLUTIONS

Progressive reformers shared the quality of optimism. They believed progress was possible—perhaps even inevitable. Activists documented problems and worked to find solutions to problems because they shared the hope that society would genuinely become better.

Labor organizers tried to work for more stability for their organizations by prioritizing the most valuable workers. The American Federation of Labor (AFL) became the most powerful labor union because it emphasized membership among skilled craftsmen who had bargaining power on the job because of the difficulty of replacing them. If, for example, you have a gang of men digging a ditch for a building, they do not have a high skill level. If they form a union and strike for higher wages, the company owner could easily fire them and hire replacements who could be trained quickly. However, if your carpenters, brick masons, and glass workers strike, they are harder to replace. You can't take a man off the street and

---

1 William A. Link, *The Paradox of Southern Progressivism, 1880–1930* (Chapel Hill: The University of North Carolina Press, 1992), 240.

show him in a few hours how to build a solid foundation. By focusing on the most valuable of the blue-collar workers, the AFL was able to make concrete gains in what they called "bread and butter" issues, like higher pay and safer working conditions. The AFL did not welcome unskilled laborers or workers with radical ideas, such as anarchists and Marxists. Increasingly, the conservative position of the AFL convinced many Americans that this type of labor activism was safe and helped created progress and stability for the working class.

The politicians of the Progressive Era tackled the problem of monopoly by trust busting. Activists worked to pass the Sherman Anti-Trust Act in 1890, which made it illegal for businesses to manipulate trade or to hold a monopoly of the market for their product. President Theodore Roosevelt (president from 1902 to 1908) and President Taft (president from 1908 to 1912) drew on this legislation to break up big companies and prevent other companies from getting too large and having too much influence over their market. For a modern-day example of trust busting, see the 1999 Microsoft case. The courts ruled that Microsoft was creating a monopoly on computer operating systems and ordered it to share the market.

At the municipal, or city level, politicians expanded the size of city government and created better systems for managing the large populations in cities. Engineers created better sanitation systems and pipelines for clean water. Police forces encouraged more training and equipment for their officers to combat crime in an effective manner. Progressive activists encouraged having more transparency in government and progressive journalists worked to expose and shame corruption in local governments. Technicians drew on the fabulous new invention of light bulbs to equip city streets with light. Overall cities became cleaner, safer, and better run thanks to the Progressive movement.

One of the most well-known institutions of the Progressive movement was the settlement house, brought to America by Stanton Coit and popularized in Chicago by Jane Addams. Jane Addams grew up in Illinois as the wealthy and well-educated daughter of a US Senator. Like a growing number of women in her generation, she went to college and excelled at her studies, but once she graduated she did not have an outlet for her talent. Like other Americans, she was aware of the growing numbers of immigrants who lived and worked in dangerous conditions. She bought a house in Chicago in an immigrant neighborhood and used her sociology education to study her neighbors and offer programs to help them. Other college-educated women joined her, and together they crafted a large variety of resources. They had classes on English, geometry, lectures on politics, exercise sessions, singing groups, and numerous other enrichment programs. Settlement house workers sometimes carried an air of condescension and cultural superiority as white women focused on assimilating immigrants to what they thought were more elevated, American ways of cooking, eating, raising children, and keeping house.

Many settlement house workers argued that women had special expertise to guide children and clean up cities, based on their supposed biological and social affinity for raising children and organizing a home. Women could draw on this special expertise to clean up cities, make children's lives better by fighting for child labor laws, expanding kindergartens, and encouraging policies to increase maternal health, and make safer working conditions for female factory workers. Some activists called this "maternal housekeeping" and also used this reasoning to argue that women should have the right to vote to help clean up the problems created by corrupt male politicians. The suffrage movement gained momentum and women ultimately won the vote nationwide when the states ratified the Nineteenth Amendment to the Constitution in 1920.

Particularly in the South, reformers targeted health, education, and child labor. One of the most popular reforms was the anti-hookworm crusade. Medical professions went from town to town with a caravan of marvels about the hookworm. People flocked to see blown-up pictures of hookworms and used microscopes to examine live eggs and larvae. Health workers tested people for infection and treated them. People recovered quickly with only a short course of medicine, and they spread the word to their neighbors. The success of this initiative helped break down traditions of localism and hostility toward outsiders, giving other health reformers a better climate for other medical initiatives. Northern philanthropists donated money to build schoolhouses and increase educational reform. Although less successful, the crusade against child labor gathered data and made important strides to tackle the problem.

Two of the most important achievements of the Progressive Era were the creation of the Food and Drug Administration and the National Parks system. Upton Sinclair, a novelist concerned about the exploitation of workers, wrote a novel, *The Jungle,* about the cruelty workers faced in the meat-packing factories of Chicago. Sinclair hoped that readers would be shocked at the brutal labor conditions and become sympathetic to socialism. Instead, readers zeroed in on the graphic descriptions of how unsanitary meat conditions were and demanded government action. The Food and Drug Administration ensured that businesses could not put profits over sanitation and regulated the cleanliness of consumer products.

Another concern raised about the growth of urban factories and cities was the increasing loss of people's connection to nature. President Roosevelt, long a believer in the healing power of the wilderness, created the national parks system to preserve natural spaces from being swallowed up by the overexploitation of natural resources. The result from Roosevelt and similar thinkers was natural treasures such as Yosemite and Yellowstone.

Progressive activists therefore made a number of important and long-lasting contributions in a wide variety of areas. Yet they did not come close to challenging the loss of the vote, racial violence, or the rising walls of segregation. So historians often and justifiably ask: *Where did African Americans fit into the Progressive Era?*

A REGRESSIVE ERA?

Most textbooks leave African Americans out of the story of the Progressive Era and compartmentalize African Americans as a southern story separate from the larger national trends. The dominant narrative of this story is the transition from slavery to freedom and the rise of the Jim Crow era.

Thanks to both enslaved people who bravely flocked to Union camps and President Lincoln's willingness to be flexible, freedom rose to the top of the agenda of the Civil War. The Emancipation Proclamation freed people in theory, northern troops freed people at the point of a gun, and slaves asserted their preference by running away from their masters. Congress passed the Thirteenth Amendment after the War and put an end to legal slavery. African Americans were free, but they were freed without resources and left helpless before the anger of their former masters. The years of Reconstruction, the period after the Civil War, saw many hopeful steps. Radical Republicans passed the Fourteenth and Fifteenth Amendments to the Constitution, guaranteeing citizenship and the vote to black men. Many African Americans found lost family members, negotiated the ability to work in family groups rather than single-sex gangs, voted, and held political office. The Freedmen's Bureau helped negotiate tensions, and the Union army provided military protection for the rights of the freedmen. But white southerners continued to fight to re-establish white supremacy. Multiple incidents of violence targeted the rights of black citizens. White southerners bitterly resented the loss of their privilege and repeatedly tried to stop African Americans from exercising their freedoms.

Unfortunately white northerners did not have the vision or resolve to protect black rights. Part of the problem was the North's widespread racism. Before the Civil War most white northerners, including Abraham Lincoln, believed that white people were physically and intellectually superior to black people. This white supremacist belief coexisted with the principle that slavery was unfair. Lincoln and other moderate republicans believed people should not be owned or sold, and definitely should be paid for their work. They also believed, perhaps above all, that slavery hurt white workers, small business owners, and farmers. Radical abolitionists who believed in racial equality and envisioned a diverse America with races living in harmony were a small percentage of the population.

However, because white southerners refused to compromise on any aspect of slavery and insisted on trying to expand slave territory to the west, moderate northerners were willing to stop them during the Civil War. During the early years of Reconstruction, as white southerners attempted to re-enslave people in all but name, Radical Republicans backed the Freedmen's Bureau, a military presence, and the Fourteenth and Fifteenth Amendments as ways of protecting African Americans from another slavery. But as the years went on, white northerners grew tired of defending black rights in the form of money for the Freedmen's Bureau and soldiers stationed in the south. Most white northerners did not, in any case, truly believe in racial equality. They increasingly reasoned that since slavery was over, the federal government should stop interfering with the South.

White southerners lost the Civil War but largely won the peace. During the last decades of the nineteenth century, white southerners across the former states of the Confederacy launched campaigns of racist terror and political trickery that destroyed the civil rights of African Americans. How could white southerners justify these actions in a nation ostensibly devoted to democracy and liberty? White supremacists argued that people of African descent were not capable of freedom. Additionally they argued that since emancipation, African Americans were actually losing ground in their state of civilization. White southerners claimed that crime and disease were increasing among the black population. Some doctors and scientists even somberly predicted that black people would die out since they could not live without the direction of slave owners.

In 1890 Mississippi rewrote its state constitution to put in barriers to voting that theoretically applied to anyone, but in reality mainly barred African Americans from voting. Soon other states of the former Confederacy followed suit. Local governments began passing laws mandating segregated public spaces. For example, African American children could not swing on swings at the local parks or swim in the local swimming pools. Waiting rooms at train stations became divided into black and white, and trains, busses, streetcars, and other forms of transportation became segregated. Brave activists like Ida B. Wells, a teacher and journalist in Memphis, Tennessee, challenged these segregation laws in court, but ultimately lost. In 1896 the Supreme Court declared in *Plessy v. Ferguson* that "separate but equal" segregation laws were legal. More than thirty years after a decisive Union victory in the Civil War ended slavery, the former Confederate states built a new architecture of white supremacy.

THE PROGRESSIVE MOVEMENT AND RACE

Most of the individuals and organizations commonly identified with the Progressive movement did very little to support black leaders tackling the rising walls of white supremacy. Trust-busting oil, steel, and other monopolies helped small businesses, workers, and consumers in industrial areas. But such actions had only a minor impact on rural sharecroppers. Southern progressives put forth great effort to fight alcohol, improve sanitation, and build school houses but did so within the confines of racial segregation. Even white southerners opposed to violence did so within a framework of white supremacy, reasoning that whites should be in charge but they should not be cruel about it. This flavor of white supremacists believed African Americans were inferior but capable of progress, and it was the Christian duty of white people to help them. Increasingly, municipal funds went to improve the white sections of towns while underfunding the rest. Black residents were often forced to live areas with the worst housing and fewest services.

At the national level, the American Federation of Labor proclaimed it was "open to all regardless of race, sex, nationality, creed, or color" but was willing to tolerate racism at the local level.[2] White southern workers often (but not always) refused to let black workers join their union, and so the gains of the labor movement passed by most African Americans.

Even organizations dominated by white women largely excluded women of color. White southern women spearheaded fundraising campaigns to celebrate the "Lost Cause" and put up monuments honoring Confederate soldiers. The nation's largest anti-alcohol group, the Women's Christian Temperance Union, had integrated northern chapters but allowed southern chapters to segregate and discriminate by race. Similarly, the suffrage movement focused on winning a national constitutional amendment for women's right to vote, knowing that black women in the South would probably be barred from it. Talented black women were sidelined by a suffrage movement that prioritized white women's right to vote over voter rights for all citizens.

AFRICAN AMERICAN ACTIVISTS

While the mainstream Progressive movement at best ignored, and at worst increased, white supremacy in America, black leaders came up with competing ideas about how to improve conditions. The great Frederick Douglass, who ran away from slavery in Maryland and spent his life writing and speaking persuasively about his love of the Constitution and

---

2 Committee on the President's AFL Convention of 1900, in *Black Workers: A Documentary History from Colonial Times to the Present*, ed. Philip Foner and Ronald L. Lewis (Philadelphia: Temple University Press, 1989), 240.

his belief that America would live up to its promises of freedom and equality for all, died in 1895 in a climate of increasing hostility. Although there were many talented African American men and women who had different perspectives on how to work to better their people, white Americans tended to look for one single leader or spokesperson for all African Americans. They wondered who would fill Frederick Douglass's place.

White southerners and northerners thought they found their answer with Booker T. Washington. Washington was born a slave in Virginia. Freed by the Civil War, he ultimately went to Hampton University, Virginia, for an education and later became the principal of an industrial school in Alabama. His school, Tuskegee Institute, offered practical courses to train men to be expert carpenters, brick masons, farmers, and other sorts of skilled craft occupations. Women who went to Tuskegee learned to be seamstresses, cooks, laundresses, and other jobs open to women. At the Cotton Exposition, a fair in Atlanta, Washington was invited to address a large crowd. White southerners at the fair hoped to attract the investment of northern businessmen. The Civil War greatly impoverished the South, and a new generation of white southerners, such as Henry Grady of Atlanta, hoped to take the South in a new direction, away from an overreliance on agricultural crops like cotton and tobacco and toward more industrial pursuits, such as textile factories. This vision was called "the New South." Proponents of this plan wanted northern industrialists to see the South as a peaceful region with plentiful natural resources and cheap labor, in the hopes that northern businessmen, flush with money from the prosperous Gilded Age, would invest in the South.

So Booker T. Washington had a tricky job at the fair, but he rose to the challenge, giving a powerful speech that brought congratulations from all groups. He promised that African Americans would be excellent workers in the southern economy and work without unions or strikes. He praised the faithfulness of former slaves who helped their masters during the Civil War, asserting that white and black southerners still had a good relationship. Additionally, he argued that the sudden gains of citizenship rights during Reconstruction had been a mistake, and that African Americans should stop working for social and political issues and concentrate on available jobs and saving up to buy their own homes and farms.

Telegrams of congratulations poured in for Washington, and many hailed him as the new leader of his race. His speech became known as the Atlanta Compromise. In a compromise, each side bargains away something they have in return for something they want. Both blacks and whites understood Washington's compromise to be giving up on full citizenship in return for economic opportunity.

Over time, Washington solidified his reputation and traveled around the country giving more speeches and meeting with political figures and heads of industry. Theodore Roosevelt admired Washington and often consulted him about potential candidates for jobs. Washington, DC, was not segregated, and so jobs like judgeships and post office heads could be filled by African American employees. Booker T. Washington had the ear of the president. Roosevelt even caused a scandal in the South when he ate lunch with Booker T. Washington, an act that breached the protocol of segregation.

But as Washington continued to preach the virtues of compromise and encouraged his model of industrial schooling, a new wave of activists began to criticize his leadership.

The fiery journalist Ida B. Wells was one of the first to openly criticize Washington. Born a slave and freed by the Civil War, Ida B. Wells worked first as a teacher and then became an influential journalist in Memphis, Tennessee. Her exposé of the falsehoods behind the defense of lynch mobs made her a target of violence. After a white mob burned her press, she relocated to the safety of the North. Wealthy, reform-minded black women in northern cities took up her cause and raised money for Wells to continue her investigative journalism. By the late 1890s, Wells grew frustrated with the accommodationism of Washington and openly criticized him in a speech and private letters. Monroe Trotter, the editor of the *Boston Guardian*, the leading black paper in Massachusetts, launched a campaign against Washington. Trotter grew up free in the north and excelled at school, earning a degree from Harvard. A clear contradiction to Washington's message that African Americans should concentrate on industrial education, Trotter used his position as editor to launch multiple written attacks on Washington and his message.

Most persuasively, William Edward Burghardt Du Bois published a scathing critique of Washington in his remarkable work, *Souls of Black Folk*, published in 1903. Du Bois was born free in Great Barrington, Massachusetts, and became the first black man to earn a doctorate from Harvard. He worked as a sociologist at Atlanta University, believing that social science research could help convince Americans of the false basis of bigotry. Du Bois criticized Washington for giving up on political rights, on prioritizing industrial schooling over a liberal arts education, and for compromising the dream of equality.

Although there were many other African American activists and leaders who worked to better their situation in the early twentieth century, the clashing visions of Du Bois and Washington dominated the debates at the time and set the framework for historians' understanding of this period. Washington preached that African Americans should get training for and work at professions that were open to them, such as farming, carpentry, mason, cooking, and other manual labors. He was pragmatic and did not see any advantage in African Americans training for and trying for jobs that were barred to them, such as medicine and law. But he argued that with a steady income from available jobs, people could buy their homes and land and become independent. With increased wealth and stability, black southerners would earn the respect of their neighbors and over time convince white southerners of their fitness for the vote and other civil rights. Additionally, working their way up peacefully would hopefully mean an end to violence, since they would be a non-threatening but important part of the southern economy.

Du Bois had an entirely different vision. He believed that this Atlanta Compromise in 1895 had not yielded any benefits by 1903 but had only given white southerners a clear conscience to keep raising higher the walls of segregation. The loss of the vote meant that white politicians had no reason to work for their black constituents, so they passed numerous laws to strengthen white supremacy. Du Bois thought that African Americans needed well-educated leaders, people who had a good liberal arts exposure so they could think broadly and expansively to come up with new solutions to the new version of oppression. Additionally, Du Bois worked as a social scientist to document the reality of black life in the South. Many white southerners and Americans believed false myths about African American nature and character. White supremacist doctors and scientists continued to expand stereotypes from slavery and proclaimed that people of African descent were lazy, not intelligent, and childlike. Southerners argued these supposed traits justified slavery before the Civil War and justified segregation afterward. Du Bois thought the power of facts and rational argument could undermine the basis for racism.

White leaders had a limited ability to recognize black talent and thus tended to acknowledge one person as the leader of all African Americans. However, there were many other African American leaders who effectively worked alone or in groups to challenge Jim Crow and improve conditions. Maggie Lena Walker, a bank president in Virginia, used her financial aptitude to increase wealth for the black community in Richmond. Other black writers worked within the muckraking spirit of progressive journalists to expose the injustices of Jim Crow. Thousands of southern sharecroppers passed around illicit copies of *The Chicago Defender*, a newspaper that celebrated black pride and gave people concrete information about how to migrate north for industrial jobs. The paper's editor, Robert Abbott, channeled his powerful voice to expose racist practices and events. In part because of the racism of white women's organizations, leading black women formed the National Association of Colored Women. This umbrella organization had an ambitious agenda that included votes for women, challenges to segregation, and better schools for black children. Black women such as Lugenia Burns Hope embraced the progressive era idea of municipal housekeeping. She helped create the Neighborhood Union, an organization that helped improve the health and education of poor children in Atlanta.

THE END OF THE PROGRESSIVE ERA, THE CONTINUATION OF THE BLACK FREEDOM STRUGGLE

Most scholars of US history acknowledge the importance of these leaders but put them in a larger framework of popular activism in the black freedom struggle rather than calling them "Progressives." In this line of reasoning, activism against segregation was both an updated version of the anti-slavery struggle and part of the early civil rights movement, rather than a distinctive era. Typically textbooks end the Progressive Era with World War I, since many Americans rallied around the flag and considered criticisms of the country unpatriotic. During the late 1910s, many progressive initiatives faltered. Trust busting gave way to a celebration of riches in the Roaring 1920s and progressives were no longer in favor. However, black activism against Jim Crow kept rising. NAACP membership swelled, and the Great Migration expanded the wealth, education, and political power of African Americans. Thus, the general consensus that the Progressive Era ended as black activism surged is another reason historians tend to separate these phenomenon; they simply seemed to be operating on tracks that ran parallel but never connected.[3]

3 A few historians have attempted to merge these segregated histories. In 1996, Glenda Gilmore argued that "it is important to make an explicit attempt to reclaim 'progressivism'" and suggested that centering black women's activism as political resistance was one way to "build a new progressivism." From *Gender and Jim Crow: Women and the Politics of White Supremacy in North Carolina, 1896–1920* (Chapel Hill: The University of North Carolina Press, 1996), 150.

A PROGRESSIVE ERA FOR ALL?

Your job is to examine the evidence and draw a conclusion about the Progressive Era.

Some questions to consider as you work through the essays and documents are the following:

1. Should we think in terms progress? Recall that African American leaders responded to white supremacists' argument that black Americans were sliding backwards after Emancipation by strenuously insisting on African American improvement. In other words, do we have even more reason to call the early twentieth century the Progressive Era if we conclude that African Americans were making progress?
2. Should we think in terms of activism? In other words, should we think of the early twentieth century as less of an era and more of a time of movement? If so, do we think African American leaders who fought against segregation were part of the Progressive movement?

After reading two short essays and delving into primary sources, it will be up to you decide: Was the early twentieth century a Progressive Era for African Americans?

TIMELINE

1889 Hull House in Chicago founded by Jane Addams and Ellen Gates Starr	**1896** William McKinley elected President Supreme Court decides in *Plessy v. Ferguson* decision that "separate but equal" is law National Association of Colored Women founded	**1901** President McKinley shot Booker T. Washington publishes autobiography *Up from Slavery*
1890 Sherman Anti-Trust Act passed by Congress Mississippi State Constitution adds literacy test and poll tax	**1897** American Negro Academy founded	**1903** W. E. B. Du Bois publishes *Souls of Black Folk*
1893 *McClure's Magazine* begins publication and becomes leading muckraking paper	**1898** Spanish American War Wilmington, North Carolina, race riot kills fourteen people and destroys local republican political power	**1904** Theodore "Teddy" Roosevelt elected president Ida Tarbell publishes *The History of the Standard Oil Company*

1905
W. E. B. Du Bois and Monroe Trotter organize the Niagara movement
Robert Abbott founds *The Chicago Defender*

1906
Upton Sinclair publishes *The Jungle*
Alpha Phi Alpha founded, the first black fraternity
Race Riot in Atlanta, Georgia

1908
Race riot in Springfield, Illinois (birthplace of Abraham Lincoln)
William Howard Taft elected president
In *Muller v. Oregon* Supreme Court allows states to limit women's working hours

1909
NAACP founded

1910
National Urban League founded

1911
Triangle Shirtwaist Fire in New York City prompts outrage and progressive action

1912
Woodrow Wilson elected president

1914
Marcus Garvey creates the Universal Negro Improvement Association

1917
United States enters World War I; Great Migration starts

1920
States ratify the Nineteenth Amendment for women's suffrage

HISTORIANS' CONVERSATIONS

POSITION #1—THE PROGRESSIVE ERA WAS THE NADIR OF AFRICAN AMERICAN HISTORY

In 1954, the historian Rayford Logan called the late nineteenth century the "nadir," or lowest point, of African American history.[1] This was a bold claim. Wasn't slavery the worst part of African American history? How could freedom be worse than slavery?

To be blunt, no matter the horrors of slavery, a slave's life was still valuable. Most slave owners had an economic incentive to protect the life of their slaves, whereas a landowner after the Civil War who employed sharecroppers could view them as replaceable at no cost. Of course, some slave owners were irrational and harmed slaves despite their economic value. But in the post–Civil War period, there was no economic check on the brutality of white southerners, who lashed out in racist violence. If landowners killed their black workers, they faced little to no consequences and could find more black workers since almost all other jobs were closed to African Americans. Slave lives mattered before the Civil War, but afterward sharecropper lives did not. Although the early twentieth century was a time of progress for white Americans, it continued many of the patterns of the late nineteenth century that caused life to be challenging for African Americans, especially in the areas of jobs, segregation, politics, and culture.

Progressive organizations did not address these challenges for rural, southern African Americans. Progressives were largely unconcerned with racial tensions and often blocked African American membership from their groups. Consequently, the concerns faced by black citizens were absent from the progressive agenda.

JOBS

The majority of African Americans in the early twentieth century worked in agriculture in the rural South. Many were sharecroppers. Sharecropping is a system where multiple participants interacted: landowners, sharecroppers, and store owners. At the end of the Civil War, white southerners had land, but little money. African Americans had freedom, but no land or money. Stores had goods, or the ability to get credit from northern merchants for goods, but few customers since so many people were impoverished by the war.

1 Rayford W. Logan, *The Negro in American Life and Thought: The Nadir, 1877–1901* (New York: Dial Press, 1954).

So southerners created a system. Store owners offered landowners a line of credit. Landowners could get seed, fertilizer, and other goods with the promise of repaying in several months when the harvest came in. Landowners then offered or compelled African Americans to live and work on their land. They were not paid an hourly wage, but were promised a *share* of the *crop* when it was harvested or sold. Sharecroppers could get supplies at the stores through the landowners' line of credit. Much of their food, clothing, medical supplies, and other items came from this store. Once the crop came in, the landowners took it to market and sold it. With the profits, they deducted what the sharecroppers owed for their supplies from the store, and then paid them the rest for their labor, depending on their agreed percentage of the crop.[2]

In theory, this system should have offered benefits to all parties in a cash-poor region. In reality, only landowners and merchants profited. Most African Americans could not read or do math, so they could be easily cheated. Often they were not given accurate, or even any, information on what the crop sold for, how much each item at the store cost, and what interest they were charged on the store debt. Often a sharecropping family would work for a year and then be told they earned no money. Even worse, they might be told they *owed* the landowner for supplies they used from the general store.

Once in debt, sharecroppers were stuck. If they tried to leave to find a better landowner or a job in a city, the police could track them down and jail them. If parents were jailed, their children could be placed in white homes, which basically made them unpaid servants. This cycle of work and debt, enforced by the criminal justice system, was called *debt peonage*.

Across the south, states had labor camps where incarcerated African Americans worked to profit others. Many of these camps were brutal and used violence to extract labor. One, Parchman Farm, has been studied extensively, and it has been revealed to be run by sadistic managers who frequently murdered their workers. A historian who studied this system called it "worse than slavery."

POLITICS

Politically, the early twentieth century was a time of loss for African Americans. After the Civil War, during Reconstruction, Congress granted the rights of citizenship and the vote. But this development was violently contested in the 1880s and 1890s. By 1900, most southern states had put up barriers to vote for African Americans. The Grandfather clause stipulated that if you or your ancestors had the right to vote before the Civil War, you did not have to meet any other requirements to vote. This meant in reality that if your grandfather was a slave, he could not have voted, and so you and all his descendants could face multiple barriers to vote. One barrier was a literacy test, with complex questions about minute details of the Constitution. Local county registrars administered the test and routinely

2 For more on labor practices, see Peter J. Rachleff, *Black Labor in the South: Richmond Virginia, 1865–1890* (Urbana: University of Illinois, 1984) and Gerald Jaynes, *Branches Without Roots: The Genesis of the Black Working Class, 1862–1888* (New York: Oxford University Press, 1986).

failed African American applicants, no matter how well they did. Poll taxes meant that only those with sufficient disposable income could vote. Slowly, black office holders disappeared. Around election time, white politicians seeking office no longer bothered to listen to black constituents or make them promises to address their concerns. They could not vote, so they had little voice or influence in politics.[3]

Nationally, white politicians and activists championed progressive causes like trust busting, safer cities, ending corruption in government, preserving the wilderness, and so on. But these progressives had little concern for African American issues.

One of the most well-known progressives, Theodore Roosevelt, president from 1901 and re-elected in 1904, avoided radical African Americans who advocated for their civil rights. He preferred the company of Booker T. Washington, who did not make demands and was willing to work within the system of segregation. Many African Americans were outraged when Roosevelt callously handled the Brownsville situation. In 1906, black soldiers were stationed in Brownsville, Texas. Proud of fighting for their country, these soldiers were insulted by the poor treatment they received from residents who thought black men should not be soldiers. One night a fight broke out and a white police officer was killed. The police blamed the black soldiers and presented evidence they were behind the murder. Later investigations showed that the soldiers were in their quarters that night. The evidence against them was flimsy and almost certainly false. President Roosevelt did not look closely into the matter, and he quickly took action to discharge over 150 black soldiers without honor, ruining their reputations personally and casting suspicion on the honor of all black soldiers. Nationally, African Americans found this shocking.[4]

In the 1912 election, Roosevelt left the Republican Party and joined a new third party that called itself the Progressive Party. But Roosevelt refused to admit black southern delegates to this party's convention, sending a clear message that the leaders of the Progressive movement turned their backs on racial equality.

Woodrow Wilson, elected in 1912 in part from support of progressives, was even more disappointing. He expanded segregation in the federal government and minimized the number of black men in federal positions. In 1914, a delegation of African Americans visited him in the White House to protest the situation. Monroe Trotter and others explained that segregation and disfranchisement were a betrayal of democracy. Wilson did not like their tone and threw them out of his office.

The Progressive movement centered on identifying problems, crafting solutions, and lobbying the government to enact reforms. Since a majority of African Americans lived in a region where they could not vote or hold office, the methods of the Progressive movement did not work for them.

---

3 For more on political challenges, see Nell Irvin Painter, *Standing at Armageddon: The United States, 1877–1919* (New York: W.W. Norton, 1987).

4 For more on the Brownsville affair and other tragedies, see David W. Southern, *The Progressive Era and Race: Reaction and Reform, 1900–1917* (Wheeling, IL: Harland Davidson, 2005).

SEGREGATION

One of the worst aspects of life in the early twentieth century was the rise of segregation. Segregation did not spring into being at the end of the Civil War with the emancipation of slaves. White supremacists were only able to pass laws once they regained control of southern politics in the 1890s. Early in the twentieth century, Jim Crow laws flourished. Local and state governments passed laws on public space, schools, and miscegenation throughout the first two decades of the twentieth century.

Progressives and segregation went hand in hand. Progressive politicians in the South believed themselves moral beings, worried about racist violence. Instead of denouncing mobs and pursuing the arrest and conviction of white supremacists who murdered African Americans, white southern progressives thought the best solution was segregation.

Part of the mentality of white progressives came from social Darwinism. Charles Darwin's book *On the Origin of Species* explained evolution and species diversity through mechanisms like natural selection and survival of the fittest. He did not say what this meant for humans. But many people began to apply these new theories to explain and justify a classification of races. White supremacists believed that Anglo-Saxons dominated the world militarily and politically because they were biologically the fittest race. The most extreme white supremacists hoped African Americans and other races they considered inferior would die out.

Thus some white southerners could consider segregation a progressive and moral solution to allow different races to live together in harmony. In this vision whites would occupy the most privileged places and have the best education, jobs, and leadership positions. African Americans could work as farmhands, maids, servants, and other menial positions. As long as everybody kept to their place, they could live together.

VIOLENCE

The boundaries of these place lines were patrolled by violence. Whites employed a spectrum of violence in the early twentieth century, but the most extreme was lynching. A lynching is when a mob (three or more people) kills another person who is accused of a crime. Lynchings were rare before the Civil War, but they increased in the late nineteenth century. With the loss of slavery, southern whites tried to create a replacement for a system of white supremacy and turned to violence to enforce their new system. Essentially, southern whites lynched African Americans to enforce the boundaries of white supremacy. If African Americans tried to vote, argue about a fair wage for their crop, run a successful business, or even walk on the wrong side of the sidewalk, they could be lynched. White southerners could accuse African Americans of serious crimes like murder, rape, or arson, and then target an accused victim for death without going through the constitutional process of trial by jury of their peers.

Lynchings could become mass spectacles, with people torturing the victim before a cheering crowd of thousands. After the murder, sometimes witnesses fought for souvenirs such as a body part or took pictures of themselves smiling by the corpse. The threat of violence hung over all life. African Americans knew if they challenged white supremacy in any way they risked their lives. African Americans appealed to the courts and politicians with little response. Ending lynching was simply not on the progressive agenda.

CULTURE

Even as African Americans lost ground in terms of political rights and public space, fictional portrayals of African Americans were hugely popular in novels, stories, and theater. White authors found audiences interested in tales of life before the Civil War and crafted numerous sketches of "happy darkies," slaves who had an easy workload, a kind master, and spent most of their time singing and dancing. White minstrels in black face were in demand as traveling performers who put on stage productions of life in the sunny south, with music and dance moves they learned from uncompensated black artists.

The popularity of these plays and stories said more about white people's desires and fears than about the reality of black life. Many white people had some genuine appreciation for black culture such as song and dance, but enjoyed a warped version of black life that emphasized leisure, a connection to nature, and unrepressed sexuality. This fictional version of black life appealed to white workers shifting to an industrial economy where they faced rigidly structured days, jobs and homes in concrete cities, and the reality that only delayed gratification of desires could help them succeed.[5]

Although some African Americans owned their own land and headed up businesses and accumulated wealth, the majority was trapped in cycles of debt and poverty and had no disposable income to spend on books, plays, or shows. Black audiences could not support black artists. So white artists, catering to white audiences, dominated the cultural landscape and crafted a version of black life that did not reflect reality. White Americans thought they knew and understood African Americans because of what they learned from culture, but they only had a distorted view. Consequently when black activists tried to expose the problems of violence and segregation, white Americans dismissed them as misguided.

CONCLUSION

Overall, the early twentieth century was one of the worst eras for African Americans. These decades witnessed unchecked racist violence, the loss of political rights, the rising walls of Jim Crow segregation, and cultural mockery. Progressive politicians and reformers were at best indifferent and at worst malicious to African Americans. This was *not* an era of progress for African Americans.

---

5 For more on white appropriation of black culture, see Eric Lott, *Love and Theft: Blackface Minstrelsy and the American Working Class* (New York: Oxford University Press, 1993) and David R. Roediger, *The Wages of Whiteness: Race and the Making of the American Working Class* (New York: Verso, 1991).

POSITION #2—AFRICAN AMERICANS EMBRACED PROGRESSIVE VISIONS AND METHODS TO LAY A FOUNDATION FOR FUTURE GAINS

It's true that the early twentieth century had many challenges for African Americans. If you focus on the mainstream Progressive movement, you will be disappointed by the lack of concern for racial justice. However, if you focus on the actions of African Americans, you can see a great deal of progress in the early twentieth century. After the bitter struggles of the post-emancipation period, African Americans worked to lay a foundation for future success.

SEGREGATED ORGANIZATIONS

Within a segregated society, black activists created an impressive number of organizations, chief of which were churches. One area of life where African Americans preferred segregation was religion. During slavery, white masters often forced their enslaved workers to worship in white churches and only hear white ministers. White theologians emphasized a version of Christianity that supported slavery. These preachers emphasized obeying the masters, turning the other cheek, loving those that hate you, and looking for your reward in heaven. All of the biblical references strengthened the institution of slavery.

After emancipation, African Americans flocked to form their own churches, where they could celebrate their own version of Christianity that emphasized their humanity. Ministers did the best they could to lead their followers with limited education and training. But by the twentieth century, ministers increasingly earned degrees at theology schools, sometimes sponsored by northern missionaries. Church officials worked to put institutions on solid financial footing with regular collections, fundraising for buildings, and other long-term projects.

Increasingly black communities could boast of well-organized congregations who worshiped in beautiful buildings led by well-educated ministers. Often black churches were the center of community life. People gathered not just for religious communion, but for meetings to discuss political issues, raise funds for members in need, and host other community groups interested in improving their life.[6]

Similarly, black schools became a source of community pride. In the south, black schools were segregated, underfunded, and subjected to white oversight. Even with those boundaries, however, black teachers and principals worked to offer increased possibilities to black children. The increase in literacy rates is one of the greatest success stories in US history. By law slaves were not allowed to be taught to read and write. So when emancipation came, only a tiny fraction of African Americans were literate. But they knew that without education whites could exploit them through the manipulation of contracts, laws, and ledgers. Freed people wanted the weapons of knowledge for themselves. Additionally, many were devoutly religious and hungered to read the Bible first hand.[7]

One of the few curious benefits of segregation was that black school children were taught by black teachers who loved them and believed in them. Despite working in substandard buildings with limited resources, teachers facilitated the mushrooming of literacy rates, and they helped African Americans gain the tools to more fully understand and fight back against the forces of injustice.

THE POWER OF JOURNALISM

An increasingly literate black population in the early twentieth century devoured black newspapers. Part of the Progressive era pattern was journalists willing to expose scandal or corruption and bring it to the attention of the public. An informed public could then take steps to solve problems, perhaps through government action. Black journalists in the early twentieth century worked within this Progressive belief. T. Thomas Fortune edited *The New York Age*, which grew in membership during the early twentieth century. In 1901, Monroe Trotter helped found the *Guardian* in Boston, and in 1905 Robert Abbott created the *Chicago Defender*. Many other major cities had a growing black population with steady jobs who could afford to support a black newspaper.[8]

These journalists interrupted the self-congratulatory feedback loop of white justification for racism. White papers explained lynching as the only way to deal with black criminals. Black papers exposed lynching as a miscarriage of justice. White papers only reported on African Americans if accused of a crime. Black papers celebrated graduations, baptisms, inventions, business successes, births, and weddings. White papers insisted

---

6 For more on religion, see Evelyn Brooks Higginbotham, *Righteous Discontent: The Women's Movement in the Black Baptist Church, 1880–1920* (Cambridge, MA: Harvard University Press, 1993) and Paul Harvey, *Redeeming the South: Religious Cultures and Racial Identities Among Southern Baptists, 1865–1925* (Chapel Hill: The University of North Carolina Press, 1997).

7 For more on education see James D. Anderson, *The Education of Blacks in the South, 1860–1935* (Chapel Hill: The University of North Carolina Press, 1988).

8 For more on journalism, see Ethan Michaeli, *The Defender: How the Legendary Black Newspaper Changed America* (Boston: Mariner Books, 2016).

that segregation worked well and African Americans were content with their place. Black papers revealed that African Americans were not satisfied with segregation and were working for a better day.

WOMEN

African American women believed in the possibility of progress and took pride in how far they had come. To understand their goals in the twentieth century, we need to look at the particular burdens they bore in the nineteenth century.

Out of all of the horrors of slavery, one of the most heartbreaking was the intrusion on the family. Before the Civil War, African American women worked in the fields, kitchens, and nurseries for the benefit of white families. Enslaved women had limited time to care for their own family, often only between sundown and sunup. Despite many brave instances of resistance, slave women also suffered sexual assault from their masters. The invention of the cotton gin meant that land as far west as eastern Texas, and as far north as southern Missouri could profitably cultivate cotton. Thus the nineteenth century began a massive wave of domestic migration. Buyers wanted young, strong field hands to send out to the frontier to break ground for new plantations. All too frequently, mothers lost their children to sale.

Across America, in city and countryside, people crafted a model of womanhood that measured women's worth by their ability to maintain a home that was clean, comfortable, and upheld religious values. Enslaved women used many creative techniques to maintain family ties and provide for their children, but struggled in vain against the vicious forces that broke apart their efforts.[9]

After emancipation, black families sought control over their own lives. Heroically, thousands of freed people took long journeys to find lost loved ones. Once settled on land as sharecroppers, many black couples decided they did not want women working full time in the fields. Instead, women wanted to raise their own children and create a home. Many white southerners and even white northerners during Reconstruction ridiculed these efforts. Those groups wanted black women in the fields to increase crop yields and profits for southern markets and northern textile factories. Black women took pride in their considerable agricultural skills, but also prized the choice to be able to improve home life for their own families.

By the twentieth century, many black women measured progress by their ability to preserve their dominion over the home. Numerous organizations provided an opportunity for women to connect with one another, celebrate their achievements, and reach out to others. The National Association of Colored Women, founded in 1896, provided an umbrella structure for other groups. Their motto, "Lifting as We Climb," broadcast their commitment to both personal progress, but also their responsibility to help the less fortunate members of their race toward progress as well.[10]

---

9 For more on women, see Stephanie J. Shaw, *What a Woman Ought to Be and Do: Black Professional Women Workers During the Jim Crow Era* (Chicago: University of Chicago Press, 1996).

10 For more on black women's activism, see Paula Giddings, *When and Where I Enter: The Impact of Black Women on Race and Sex in America* (New York: W. Morrow, 1984).

Elite black women with education and money did not rest on their achievements, but reached out to improve the lives of others. Mary McLeod Bethune started the Literary and Industrial Training School for Girls in Florida in 1904. The school grew in size and ambition. Bethune successfully garnered donations from heads of industry such as John D. Rockefeller, and her school thrived. In 1908, Lugenia Burns Hope helped found the Neighborhood Union in Atlanta. She and other women conducted surveys of poor neighborhoods and organized volunteers to help improve sanitation, health education, and safer play areas for children. In 1909, Nannie Helen Burroughs founded the National Training School for Women and Girls in Washington, DC, that offered professional classes for black women to become highly skilled in domestic work so they could be economically self-sufficient.

These efforts of African American women are often left out of traditional accounts of the Progressive Era, but they exemplify key virtues of the traditional progressives. Club women identified problems, particularly those in cities, worked in organizations to create solutions, partnered with government agencies to find common ground, and helped make industrial habitats more livable. Although barred from the vote by race and sex, African American club women were nevertheless able to influence the political process to improve the quality of life for African Americans in cities.

BUSINESS

Although the majority of African Americans worked in rural agriculture, a growing number of enterprising individuals found success in the business world. In 1900, Booker T. Washington and other ambitious men founded the National Negro Business League, an organization that brought business men together to improve their access to and understanding of markets. Madame C. J. Walker became a millionaire selling hair care products. Maggie Lena Walker steered the Order of St. Luke's into a profitable banking enterprise. Durham Insurance grew to become one of the largest insurance companies in the country.

TUSKEGEE INSTITUTE

Though Booker T. Washington and his formula for success were controversial, almost everyone agreed that Tuskegee Institute was a source of pride and progress. The school was devoted to teaching students practical trades along segregated lines. Yet within those boundaries the school did a great deal of good for thousands of people. Graduates consistently found steady jobs. The famous scientist George Washington Carver carried out numerous experiments there that improved the lives of all Americans. Keep in mind—the man invented peanut butter. Carver held yearly farming conventions to showcase the latest updates on how to fertilize soil, use the best seed, and other ways of farming most effectively and profitably. After noting the worn-out appearance of many farm houses, Carver developed a cheap source of paint and marketed it to those in the surrounding area. Carver never patented his work. A deeply religious and thoughtful man, he credited God with all of his inspirations and thought it would be wrong to personally profit from them. Additionally, he wanted his works to help his people live better lives. Thanks to Tuskegee Institute, Alabama families had a place to send their children to master a marketable trade.

Struggling farmers had access to the latest agricultural knowledge in order to keep their farms profitable, and they could even beautify their homes with Carver's paint.[11]

Margaret Murray Washington created the Tuskegee Women's Club, a group of female teachers at Tuskegee and the wives of male teachers. Together the members worked with women in the surrounding countryside to help improve their ability to care for their children and houses. Additionally, Margaret Murray Washington worked with other people to successfully convince the criminal justice system to take juvenile offenders into their custody instead of going to prison.

Until his death in 1915, Booker T. Washington remained an effective champion of Tuskegee Institute. He traveled the country giving speeches on the merits of the school and the successes of its graduates. Captains of industry such as Andrew Carnegie found Washington convincing, and they donated money to the school and to other institutions aimed at aiding African Americans.

THE NATIONAL ASSOCIATION FOR THE ADVANCEMENT OF COLORED PEOPLE

Perhaps the most well-known step toward progress in the early twentieth century was the formation of the National Association for the Advancement of Colored People (NAACP). After the Civil War, most white-dominated abolitionist groups disbanded, considering their mission accomplished. Black leaders made numerous attempts to create all-black activist groups dedicated to progress, such as the Niagara movement. These groups did a great deal of good and connected important intellectuals to one another. But overall the members did not have the financial resources to challenge white supremacy. But this changed after the 1908 riot in Springfield, Illinois. Horrified at the spread of the southern lynching mentality to the Midwest, even in the birthplace of Abraham Lincoln, a number of white activists, many descendants of abolitionists, reached out to black activists to form an organization dedicated to challenging white supremacy. They called their organization the NAACP and worked to create a "beloved community" where blacks and whites lived together in love and harmony.

Their goal was integration. It is hard today to realize how radical such a goal was. Many people are aware of the dramatic gains of the civil rights movement of the 1950s and 1960s, the rising gains for all races, and the election of President Obama. We do not have a fully equal society today, but certainly most Americans agree that integration is a workable and desirable goal. This was not the case for a majority of white and black Americans in the early twentieth century. Black Americans argued over multiple possibilities for progress such as integration but also segregation on a large scale, such as setting aside the black belt region of the south for black residents, all-black towns within majority white states, and most extreme, migration back to Africa. Many white Americans thought integration was not possible or desirable, and some of the most liberal thought that the best solution was a sympathetic version of segregation, where African Americans were unequal but treated with kindness.

---

11 For more on Washington, see Robert J. Norrell, *Up from History: The Life of Booker T. Washington* (Cambridge, MA: Belknap Press, 2009).

Integration, then, was a radical goal. The NAACP had financial resources from wealthy white members, and it focused on challenging America to live up to the promises made during Reconstruction of full and equal citizenship for all. They funded a magazine, *The Crisis*, to publicize outrages such as lynching and discrimination. Their board was able to hire lawyers to challenge segregation in court. Most important, they offered hope to the many throughout the country. Their membership ranks grew, and membership fees funded more investigative reports and more lawsuits. Articles in *The Crisis* plus other pamphlets and fliers caught the eyes of white liberals who donated more money. Ultimately, the NAACP's legal team grew and laid a solid foundation of legal challenges that would ultimately topple Jim Crow. Overall, the organization helped make the integration of races a foundational American value.

CONCLUSION

Overall, if you look at African American activism, you can see clear signs of progress in the early twentieth century. African Americans increased education levels and built powerful organizations like clubs and churches. With rising incomes and literacy rates, black citizens supported more newspapers. Black journalists could earn a living investigating and exposing the injustices of Jim Crow and celebrate black achievements. Women worked in organizations to improve conditions for children and increase the health and safety of cities. Although Booker T. Washington and W. E. B. Du Bois disliked each other, both became powerful voices that influenced change on multiple fronts. Though blocked from most mainstream progressive organizations, African Americans used the tools of the progressive movement. They studied problems with academic rigor, exposed them through media, and laid a foundation for later triumphs against oppression. The progressive movement did not believe in African Americans, but African Americans believed in the progressive movement.

DEBATING THE QUESTION

INTRODUCTION

ABOUT THIS SEGMENT

As you use this section to answer the Big Question, it is highly recommended that you start with the Case Study on African American leaders and work through those four documents. These writings debate the most important issues for African Americans in this time period. After evaluating these four, you can use the subject tags to choose other documents in this segment to follow up on particular themes.

On Terminology: Over the years, people have used different terms to refer to people of African descent. Some of these documents contain terms that are considered insulting today, but they were not at the time. For example, African Americans might refer to themselves and others as Negro, Black, Race Men, or Race Women, and those terms were meant to convey a sense of pride in their heritage and collective action for justice. I left all terms as they originally appeared.

DID AFRICAN AMERICAN LEADERS THINK THEY WERE MAKING PROGRESS IN THE PROGRESSIVE ERA?

This section contains documents from four black leaders who debate the quality of black life during the Progressive Era. First, Mary Church Terrell explains in 1904 why she thinks African American women have made great progress since emancipation. Next are three pieces from 1910 that are in conversation with one another. Booker T. Washington, an industrial school principal in Alabama, gave a speech in England with an optimistic view of the many positive developments he saw happening. W. E. B. Du Bois, a Harvard-trained sociologist and one of the founders of the NAACP, wrote a rebuttal to Washington and asked a number of leading activists to sign it. One of the few who did not, the novelist and stenographer Charles Chesnutt, wrote a thoughtful letter to Du Bois explaining his objections. These exchanges give us a glimpse into the conversation among black leaders. What grounds did they have for optimism or pessimism in the Progressive Era?

GUIDING QUESTIONS:

1. To what extent do authors see progress? To what extent do authors see areas of concern?
2. Before the 1960s people did not talk openly about sexual issues but only alluded to them with delicate language and coded words such as "purity" and "morality." See if you can read carefully to find places where authors make reference to sexual issues.
3. Keep track of the back-and-forth points made by Washington, Du Bois, and Chesnutt, and evaluate how convincing you find their arguments.

1.1 MARY CHURCH TERRELL, "THE PROGRESS OF COLORED WOMEN," SPEECH FROM 1904

Mary Church Terrell grew up in Memphis, Tennessee, the daughter of a wealthy man who encouraged her education. She went to college at Oberlin and excelled as a student, becoming widely admired for her intellect and commitment to social justice. Active in the women's club movement, she became the first president of the National Association of Colored Women. For most of her life she was an educator at the M Street High School in Washington, DC. The following document is her reflection on the progress made by African American women.

When one considers the obstacles encountered by colored women in their effort to educate and cultivate themselves, since they became free, the work they have accomplished and the progress they have made will bear favorable comparison, at least with that of their more fortunate sisters, from whom the opportunity of acquiring knowledge and the means of self-culture have never been entirely withheld. Not only are colored women with ambition and aspiration handicapped on account of their sex, but they are almost everywhere baffled and mocked because of their race. Not only because they are women, but because they are colored women, are discouragement and disappointment meeting them at every turn. But in spite of the obstacles encountered, the progress made by colored women along many lines appears like a veritable miracle of modern times. Forty years ago for the great masses of colored women, there was no such thing as home. Today in each and every section of the country there are hundreds of homes among colored people, the mental and moral tone of which is as high and as pure as can be found among the best people of any land.

To the women of the race may be attributed in large measure the refinement and purity of the colored home. The immorality of colored women is a theme upon which those who know little about them or those who maliciously misrepresent them love to descant. Foul aspersions upon the character of colored women are assiduously circulated by the press of certain sections and especially by the direct descendants of those who in years past were responsible for the moral degradation of their female slaves. And yet, in spite of the fateful heritage of slavery, even though the safeguards usually thrown around maidenly youth and innocence are in some sections entirely withheld from colored girls, statistics compiled by men not inclined to falsify in favor of my race show that immorality among the colored women of the United States is not so great as among women with similar environment and temptations in Italy, Germany, Sweden and France.

Scandals in the best colored society are exceedingly rare, while the progressive game of divorce and remarriage is practically unknown.

From Manning Marable, Leith Mullings, et al., *Let Nobody Turn Us Around: Voices of Resistance, Reform, and Renewal: An African American Anthology* (Lanham, MD: Rowman and Littlefield, 2003), 181–184.

The intellectual progress of colored women has been marvelous. So great has been their thirst for knowledge and so Herculean their efforts to acquire it that there are few colleges, universities, high and normal schools in the North, East and West from which colored girls have not graduated with honor. In Wellesley, Vassar, Ann Arbor, Cornell and in Oberlin, my dear alma mater, whose name will always be loved and whose praise will always be sung as the first college in the country broad, just and generous enough to extend a cordial welcome to the Negro and to open its doors to women on an equal footing with the men, colored girls by their splendid records have forever settled the question of their capacity and worth. The instructors in these and other institutions cheerfully bear testimony to their intelligence, their diligence and their success.

As the brains of colored women expanded, their hearts began to grow. No sooner had the heads of a favored few been filled with knowledge than their hearts yearned to dispense blessings to the less fortunate of their race. With tireless energy and eager zeal, colored women have worked in every conceivable way to elevate their race. Of the colored teachers engaged in instructing our youth it is probably no exaggeration to say that fully eighty percent are women. In the backwoods, remote from the civilization and comforts of the city and town, colored women may be found courageously battling with those evils which such conditions always entail. Many a heroine of whom the world will never hear has thus sacrificed her life to her race amid surroundings and in the face of privations which only martyrs can bear.

Through the medium of their societies in the church, beneficial organizations out of it and clubs of various kinds, colored women are doing a vast amount of good. It is almost impossible to ascertain exactly what the Negro is doing in any field, for the records are so poorly kept. This is particularly true in the case of the women of the race. During the past forty years there is no doubt that colored women in their poverty have contributed large sums of money to charitable and educational institutions as well as to the foreign and home missionary work. Within the twenty-five years in which the educational work of the African Methodist Episcopal Church has been systematized, the women of that organization have contributed at least five hundred thousand dollars to the cause of education. Dotted all over the country are charitable institutions for the aged, orphaned and poor which have been established by colored women. Just how many it is difficult to state, owing to the lack of statistics bearing on the progress, possessions and prowess of colored women.

Up to date, politics have been religiously eschewed by colored women, although questions affecting our legal status as a race are sometimes agitated by the most progressive class. In Louisiana and Tennessee colored women have several times petitioned the legislatures of their respective states to repel the obnoxious Jim-Crow laws. Against the convict-lease system, whose atrocities have been so frequently exposed of late, colored women here and there in the South are waging a ceaseless war. So long as hundreds of their brothers and sisters, many of whom have committed no crime or misdemeanor whatever, are thrown into cells whose cubic contents are less than those of a good size grave, to be overworked, underfed and only partially covered with vermin infested rags, and so long as children are born to the women in these camps who breathe the polluted atmosphere of these dens of horror and vice from the time they utter their first cry in the world till they are released from their suffering by death, colored women who are working for the emancipation and elevation of their race know where their duty lies. By constant agitation of this painful and hideous subject, they hope to touch the conscience of the country, so that this stain upon its escutcheon shall be forever wiped away.

Alarmed at the rapidity with which the Negro is losing ground in the world of trade, some of the farsighted women are trying to solve the labor question, so far as it concerns the women at least, by urging the establishment of schools of domestic science wherever means therefore can be secured. Those who are interested in this particular work hope and believe that if colored women and girls are thoroughly trained in domestic service, the boycott which has undoubtedly been placed upon them in many sections of the country will be removed. With so few vocations open to the Negro and with the labor organizations increasingly hostile to him, the future of the boys and girls of the race appears to some of our women very foreboding and dark.

The cause of temperance has been eloquently espoused by two women, each of whom has been appointed national superintendent of work among colored people by the Women's Christian Temperance Union. In business, colored women have had signal success. There is in Alabama a large milling and cotton business belonging to and controlled by a colored woman, who has sometimes as many as seventy-five men in her employ. Until a few years ago the principal ice plant of Nova Scotia was owned and managed by a colored woman, who sold it for a large amount. In the professions there are dentists and doctors whose practice is lucrative and large. Ever since a book was published in 1773 entitled "Poems on Various Subjects, Religious and Moral by Phillis Wheatley, Negro Servant of Mr. John Wheatley," of Boston, colored women have given abundant evidence of literary ability. In sculpture we were represented by a woman whose chisel Italy has set her seal of approval; in painting by one of Bouguereau's pupils and in music by young women holding diplomas from the best conservatories in the land. In short, to use a thought of the illustrious Frederick Douglass, if judged by the depths from which they have come, rather than by the heights to which those blessed with centuries of opportunities have attained, colored women need not hang their heads in shame. They are slowly but surely making their way up to the heights, wherever they can be scaled. In spite of handicaps and discouragements they are not losing heart. In a variety of ways they are rendering valiant service to their race. Lifting as they climb, onward and upward they go struggling and striving and hoping that the buds and blossoms of their desires may burst into glorious fruition ere long. Seeking no favors because of their color nor charity because of their needs they knock at the door of Justice and ask for an equal chance.

1.2 BOOKER T. WASHINGTON, "ON THE RACE PROBLEM IN AMERICA"

Booker T. Washington, born a slave in West Virginia, walked over 300 miles to Hampton University and worked his way through school as a janitor. A star pupil, his teachers recommended him for the job of principal at an industrial school in Tuskegee, Alabama. Under Washington's leadership, Tuskegee Institute grew and educated numerous men and women for skilled work, such as carpentry and masonry for the men, and cooking and sewing for the women. Although some white southerners thought Washington too radical, the majority thought he was taking African Americans in the right direction, training them to do menial jobs without challenging white supremacy. Northern industrial heads, such as Andrew Carnegie, admired Washington and donated money to his school. Washington increasingly became known as the spokesperson of his people, and he advised Teddy Roosevelt on political matters. In 1910, Washington went to England to study the working poor and see how they compared with those of America. He gave an interview to a newspaper reporter that contains his view on the status of African Americans.

NEW YORK, THURS. SEPT. 22, 1910

NEW YORK AGE

"WASHINGTON ON RACE PROBLEM IN AMERICA"

With regard to the racial problems in America, I know that some writers draw alarmist pictures, but, while I do not care to prophesy, I will say this, that I look *forward* to the future with hope and confidence. We have in the United States about ten million Negroes—nine million in the South and one million in the North. Well, any one who lives in the South, where the black men are so numerous, knows that the situation, so far from becoming more difficult or dangerous, becomes more and more reassuring.

In America as in Europe and elsewhere, the worst happenings are those that get talked about. The papers will be full of some story about a Negro being lynched, but they occupy themselves very little with such matters as the building of colleges or the organization of banks and other great industrial concerns by members of the Negro race. Forty-five years ago, when the race was emancipated, there were only two per cent of the Negroes who could read and write, and of course, they owned practically no property. Now education is general among them, while their material prosperity is remarkable and is constantly increasing. I cannot give you the figures for all the South States, but in two of them—Georgia and Virginia—the properties of the colored people and the white people are assessed separately, and the assessments therefore afford valuable data. Last year the colored people in Virginia owned 52,000 acres and in Georgia about 16,000 acres.

From "Washington on Race Problem in America," *New York Age* (Thursday, September 22, 1910), 1, https://newscomwc.newspapers.com/image/33451890/?terms=new%2Byork%2Bage%2B%22Booker%2BT.%2BWashington%22&pqsid=jfWoSMIRQgsiuXYbURyKvA%3A239000%3A1547124892

Again, the statistics show that the colored people in the Southern States now own over 300,000 farms that their taxable property is increasing at the rate of $12,000,000 a year. The fact is that the Southern States of the Union offer to the Negro a better chance than almost any other country in the world, both as regards skilled and unskilled labor.

NO FRICTION IN BUSINESS

The Negroes are employed by the best white people in practically every occupation. There is not, in business matters at least, practically any friction between the two races. Negroes may run real estate agencies or factories or banks and they are patronized by blacks and whites alike.

I cannot tell you whether it is true, as has been sometimes asserted, that the black race is increasing faster than the white race. The black race is undoubtedly increasing, but the increase is quite natural. With regard to the white race, the increase is swollen by immigration, while there are very few black immigrants nowadays. I do not know enough of the Negro Problem in South Africa to speak with authority on the subject, but I know that it has different aspects from that problem as it exists in America. The Negro in America is civilized, and therefore he has many needs the same as the white man. If you want to elevate a race you must raise its standard of living. You must create desires in it. No man will work except with the object of ministering to his own requirements. All I will say with regard to South Africa is this, that I think the same policy has got to be pursued there as we are pursuing in America. The Negro in America has his weaknesses and sometimes his vices, but as a rule he works. In time, no doubt, if he is properly taught, the Negro in South Africa will do the same.

In America, as I have said, the business relations between the Negroes and the white men are very close; in South Africa they are not. But there are signs of a change even in South Africa. Mr. Dube, a South African native, who was at my institute at Tuskegee, where he greatly distinguished himself, has founded a similar school on a smaller scale in Natal. I have said, and I repeat, that I look forward with confidence to the future. The racial feeling in America is not nearly so strong as many persons imagine. I have been recently on a lecturing tour through the Southern States in order to further the course of the education of the Negroes, and the large meetings I have addressed in halls, in theatres, at railways stations, and elsewhere were composed almost equally of black and white people. I may add, too, that white people have contributed handsomely towards the expenses of the campaign.

You may depend upon it that things will right themselves in due course without there being any necessity for the African race to return to the country of their ancestors. During recent years very few Negroes have gone to Liberia, probably not a hundred a year. The Negro has a sort of sentimental attachment to that vast continent from which his race sprang just as the Jew holds the East in reverence. But the black man in America no more wants to go to Africa than the Jew wants to go to Palestine.

1.3 W. E. B. DU BOIS APPEALS TO ENGLAND AND EUROPE

William Edward Burghardt Du Bois was born free in Great Barrington, Massachusetts. Extremely bright and ambitious, he earned his doctorate at Harvard University, studied in Germany, and taught sociology at Atlanta University in Georgia. Convinced that once people knew the facts they would relinquish racist stereotypes, Du Bois threw his considerable energy into studying prejudice and black life to prove that there was no rational basis for racism. After years of expanding the field of sociology, Du Bois's work came to a halt. Walking down the street one day, he saw the severed knuckles of a black man on display in a shop window. This grisly souvenir of lynching stunned the academic so much that he lost his faith in the power of knowledge. He turned his sights on activism, moved to New York City, and helped found the National Association for the Advancement of Colored People (NAACP). There he edited their magazine *The Crisis* and brought public attention to outrages against black citizens. The NAACP worked with lawyers and politicians to help expose the hypocrisy of American ideals. Although initially proud of Washington's success as an educator, Du Bois became increasingly critical of Washington's public statements, particularly his lack of engagement with the excesses of white supremacy.

AN APPEAL TO ENGLAND AND EUROPE

HEADQUARTERS—NATIONAL NEGRO COMMITTEE

20, VESEY STREET, NEW YORK, U.S.A.

OCTOBER 26TH, 1910

TO THE PEOPLE OF GREAT BRITAIN AND EUROPE

The undersigned Negro-Americans have heard, with great regret, the recent attempt to assure England and Europe that their condition in America is satisfactory. They sincerely wish that such were the case, but it becomes their plain duty to say that if Mr. Booker T. Washington, or any other person, is giving the impression abroad that the Negro problem in America is in process of satisfactory solution, he is giving an impression which is not true.

We say this without personal bitterness toward Mr. Washington. He is a distinguished American and has a perfect right to his opinions. But we are compelled to point out that Mr. Washington's large financial responsibilities have made him dependent on the rich charitable public and that, for this reason, he has for years been compelled to tell, not the whole truth, but that part of it which certain powerful interest in America wish to appear as the whole truth.

In flat contradiction, however, to the pleasant pictures thus pointed out, let us not forget that the consensus of opinion among eminent European scholars who know the race problem

From National Negro Committee (WEB Du Bois), "An Appeal to England and Europe," New York, 1910. Courtesy of the Department of Special Collections, Stanford University Libraries, M1032 Herbert Aptheker Papers, box 183, folder 21.

in America, from De Tocqueville down to Von Halle, De Laveleys, Archer and Johnston, is that it forms the gravest of American problems.

We Black men who live and suffer under present conditions and who have no reason, and refuse to accept reasons, for silence, can substantiate this unanimous testimony.

Our people were emancipated in a whirl of passion, and then left naked to the mercies of their enraged and impoverished ex-masters. As our sole means of defence we were given the ballot, and we used it so as to secure the real fruits of the War. Without it, we would have returned to slavery; with it we struggled toward freedom. No sooner, however, had we rid ourselves of nearly two-thirds of our illiteracy, and accumulated $600,000,000 worth of property in a generation, than this ballot, which had become increasingly necessary to the defence of our civil and property rights, was taken from us by force and fraud.

To-day in eight States where the bulk of the Negroes live, Black men of property and university training can be, and usually are, by law denied the ballot, while the most ignorant White man votes. This attempt to put the personal and property rights of the best of the Blacks at the absolute political mercy of the worst of the Whites is spreading each day.

Along with this has gone a systematic attempt to curtail the education of the Black race. Under a widely advertised system of "universal" education, not one Black boy in three to-day has in the United States a chance to learn to read and write. The proportion of school funds due to Black children are often spent on Whites, and the burden on private charity to support education, which is a public duty, has become almost intolerable.

In every walk of life we meet discrimination based solely on race and color, but continually and persistently misrepresented to the world as the natural difference due to condition.

We are, for instance, usually forced to live in the worst quarters, and our consequent death-rate is noted as a race trait and reason for further discrimination. When we seek to buy property in better quarters we are sometimes in danger of mob violence, or, as now in Baltimore, of actual legislation to prevent.

We are forced to take lower wages for equal work, and our standard of living is then criticised. Fully half the labour unions refuse us admittance, and then claim that as "scabs" we lower the price of labour.

A persistent caste proscription seeks to force us and confine us to menial occupations where the conditions of work are worst.

Our women in the South are without protection in law and custom, and are then derided as lewd. A widespread system of deliberate public insult is customary, which makes it difficult, if not impossible, to secure decent accommodation in hotels, railways trains, restaurants and theatres, and even in the Christian Church we are in most cases given to understand that we are unwelcome unless segregated.

Worse than all this is the wilful miscarriage of justice in the courts. Not only have 3,500 Black men been lynched publicly by mobs in the last twenty-five years without semblance or pretence of trial, but regularly every day throughout the South the machinery of the courts is used, not to prevent crime and correct the wayward among Negroes, but to wreak public dislike and vengeance, and to raise public funds. This dealing in crime as a means of public revenue is a system well-nigh universal in the South, and while its glaring brutality through private lease has been checked, the underlying principle is still unchanged.

Everywhere in the United States the old democratic doctrine of recognising fitness wherever it occurs is losing ground before a reactionary policy of denying preferment in political or industrial life to competent men if they have a trace of Negro blood, and of using the weapons of public insult and humiliation to keep such men down. It is to-day a universal demand in the South that on all occasions social courtesies shall be denied any person of known Negro descent, even to the extent of refusing to apply the titles of "Mr.," "Mrs.," and "Miss."

Against this dominant tendency strong and brave Americans, White and Black, are fighting, but they need, and need sadly, the moral support of England and of Europe in this crusade for the recognition of manhood, despite adventitious differences of race, and it is like a blow in the face to have one, who himself suffers daily insult and humiliation in America, give the impression that all is well. It is one thing to be optimistic, self-forgetful and forgiving, but it is quite a different thing, consciously or unconsciously, to misrepresent the truth.

(Signed)

J. Max Barber, B.A., Editor of *The Voice of the Negro*

C.E. Bentley, formerly Chairman of Dental Clinics, St. Louis Exposition

W. Justin Carter, Barrister, Harrisburg, Pa.

S.L. Corrothers, D.D., Pastor American M.E. Zion Church Washington, D.C.

George W. Crawford, B.A., LL.B., Barrister, formerly Clerk of Court, New Haven, Ct.

James R.L. Diggs, M.A., President of Virginia Seminary and College, Va.

W.E. Burghardt Du Bois, PhD., Author of "Souls of Black Folk," &c., Fellow of the American Association for the Advancement of Science, Member of International Law Society and Secretary of the National Afro-American Committee

Arhibald H. Grimke, late U.S. Consul to San Domingo

N.B. Marshall, B.A., LL.B., Barrister, St. Paul, Minn.

G.W. Mitchell, B.A., LL.B, Barrister, Philadelphia

Clement G. Morgan, B.A., LL. B., Barrister, formerly Alderman of Cambridge, Mass.

Edward H. Morris, Grand Master of the Grand United Order of Odd Fellows in America

N.F. Mossell, M.D., Medical Director of Douglass Hospital, Philadelphia, Pa.

James L. Neill. Recording Secretary of the National Independent League.

William Pickens, B.A. Professor of Latin, Talladega College, Ala.

William A. Sinclair, Author of "The Aftermath of Slavery," and Field Secretary of the Constitution League, which represents nine-tenths of the American Negroes, and has 15,000 coloured Ministers in affiliated relations with it.

Harry C. Smith, Editor of *The Cleveland Gazette*, for six years Member of the Legislature of Ohio.

B.S. Smith, Barrister, formerly Assistant States Attorney, State of Kansas.

William Monroe Trotter, B.A., Editor of *The Boston Guardian*

J. Milton Waldron, D.D., Pastor of Shiloh Baptist Church, Washington, D.C.

Owen M. Waller, M.D., Physician, Brooklyn, New York.

Alexander Walters, D.D., Bishop of the African M.E. Zion Church

1.4 CHARLES CHESNUTT TURNS DOWN DU BOIS'S APPEAL

Charles Chesnutt (1858–1932) was born in Ohio and raised in North Carolina. He became a financially successful court stenographer in Cleveland but dreamed of becoming a novelist. In his spare time he wrote and published short stories that caught the attention of Walter Hines Page, a prominent journalist. Chesnutt carefully saved up enough money to give himself two years for his dream. He quit his job to write full time. During this period he wrote *The Marrow of Tradition* and other works, but unfortunately he was not able to make enough money for writing to remain his full-time career. Reluctantly, he went back to stenography. Other black leaders and activists enjoyed Chesnutt's literature and respected his talented intellect. Du Bois asked Chesnutt to sign his *Appeal* criticizing Washington. In this private letter Chesnutt turns down Du Bois and explains his reasons why.

Nov. 21, 1910

My dear Dr. Du Bois:

I have your letter of November 15, enclosing copy of paper entitled "Race Relations in the United States," and asking whether I would care to sign it. In view of the very close relations of members of my family with Tuskegee—my son is in Mr. Washington's office, one of my daughters has taught there for several summers, and another was Mrs. Washington's visitor for a number of weeks this year—and in view further of the fact that I am a nominal member of the Committee of Twelve and signed my name to Mr. Washington's latest appeal for an increase of the Tuskegee endowment, I question whether it would be quite in good taste for me to sign what in effect is in the nature of an impugnment of Mr. Washington's veracity, or at least which it would be only human in him to look upon in the light of a personal attack.

As to the merits of the case—I have read the interview in the *London Morning Post*, which I presume is the expression of Mr. Washington's upon which the protest is based. After all, it is only the ordinary optimistic utterance, to which we are all well accustomed. Mr. Washington is a professional optimist, avowedly so. I imagine the English as well as the Americans understand this fact and take his statements with a grain of salt. The utterances of Mr. Archer, Sir Harry Johnston and Mr. H.G. Wells would indicate that the English understand the situation pretty thoroughly. But after all, it is largely a matter of the point of view. Mr. Washington says in that interview, "The Negro problem in the United State will right itself in time"; this I think we all hope and believe to be the fact. He says further, "I believe that when America comes to a more accurate understanding of the difficulties which the masses of the working people in other parts of the world have to struggle against it, it will have gone far towards solving what is called the race problem." I see nothing wrong about that; it is a philosophic reflection which ought to have a great deal of truth in it.

Letter from Charles W. Chesnutt to W. E. B. Du Bois, November 21, 1910, in *An Exemplary Citizen: Letters of Charles W. Chesnutt 1906–1932*, ed. Jesse S. Crisler, Robert C. Leitz III, and Joseph R. McElrath Jr. (Stanford, CA: Stanford University Press, 2002), 81–84.

He says further with regard to the racial problem in America, "I know that some writers draw alarmist pictures, but I look forward to the future with hope, and confidence." Well, I think we all look forward to the future with hope, though the degree of confidence varies so far as the immediate future is concerned. Mr. Washington says further, "any one who lives in the South, where the black men are so numerous, knows that the situation, so far from becoming more difficult or dangerous, becomes more and more reassuring." This is a matter of opinion, and Mr. Washington lives in the South, while not more than one or two of the signers of the protest do, unless Washington [D.C.] be regarded as part of the South. Personally, I have not been any farther South than Washington [D.C.] but once in twenty-seven years.

Mr. Washington says in this interview that "in America as in Europe and elsewhere the worst happenings are those that get talked about." You have recently published a newspaper letter in which the same statement is made (apropos of the condition of the colored soldiers in the west). Mr. Washington's statement in this interview about the business relations of white and black people is, I think, a little optimistic, but he knows more about them than I do. "Great industrial concerns" is rather a large term to apply to such ventures among people; the recent failure of the True Reformers is a case in point. "The racial feeling in America is not nearly so strong as many persons imagine." This may or not be true; I should like to think that it is. On the whole, if the protest is based solely on this interview, it hardly seems sufficient to bear it out.

If I were inclined to criticize the wording of the protest, I might ask, does it not lean too far the other way; is it not at least equally as pessimistic as Mr. Washington's interview was optimistic? Nowhere does Mr. Washington say that the condition of the Negro in the United States is satisfactory. The protest says among other things that "because of his dependence on the rich charitable people, he has been compelled to tell, not the whole truth but that part of it which certain powerful interests in America wish to appear as the whole truth." Admitting the fact, is the reason clear? If the word "interests" is used in the ordinary sense of political magazine controversy, I am unable to imagine what "powerful interests" could wish to keep the Negro down. The statement is at least a little obscure.

Mr. Washington does not deny in terms that the Negro problem is the greatest of American problems; it is quite consistent with its gravity that conditions should be improved. The statement that "black men of property and university training can be, and usually are, by law denied the ballot" is scarcely correct. They are in many cases denied the ballot, but hardly "by law," as covered by Mr. Ray Stannard Baker's article in the November *Atlantic*, which I read with interest.

There is, it seems to be, a little inconsistency in another respect. In one place the protest states, "No sooner had we rid ourselves of nearly two-thirds of our illiteracy," etc., than the ballot was taken away. Is it true that even in the very narrowest sense of the term illiteracy as used in the census, namely the mere ability of read and write, two-thirds of the Negroes had reached that point fifteen years ago? In a later statement it is stated that "not one black boy in three in the United Stated has a chance to learn to read and write." This may be true, but if so, it shows in comparison with the former statement a very disastrous falling off. Mr. Washington states in his interview that education is "general"; he does not state that it is universal—as it ought to be. I think that the statement about our women in the South is a little broad. Also the statement about the courts. The wording of the protest would seem to imply that universally throughout the South the courts are used "not to prevent crime and to correct the wayward among Negroes, but to wreak public dislike and vengeance, and to raise public funds." I should hate to think that this is true. Negroes, as we all know, do not always, perhaps rarely, get equal justice in the courts, especially where the question of race is involved. But it would be a libel on humanity to charge all the courts of always having such an attitude of mind. The collection of revenue by levying fines is not confined to the South; it is a practice of criminal law everywhere, and our police courts are largely used as a means of revenue North as well as South.

The protest speaks of Mr. Washington suffering daily insult and humiliation. Insult and humiliation are largely subjective, a matter of personal feeling, and I have no idea that Mr. Washington feels himself daily insulted and humiliated. Whether he ought to is a question. As a fact, I imagine he thinks that he is daily honored and uplifted. It is possible that, visiting a foreign country as a distinguished American, he may have thought that the reception accorded to colored Americans visiting Europe would not be improved by making such a statement as that contained in the appeal. We know that our rights in the North are affected by the knowledge of the North of the manner in which we are treated in the South. Possibly Mr. Washington may have been, consciously or unconsciously influenced by such a point of view. Moreover, the protest is signed by a number of gentlemen, most of whom hold or have held positions of honor and profit, political and otherwise, which they certainly could not have attained without the good will and sense of justice of white people, however imperfect that sense of justice may be in some other respects.

I have always believed that the Negro in the South will never get his rights until there is a party, perhaps a majority, of southern white

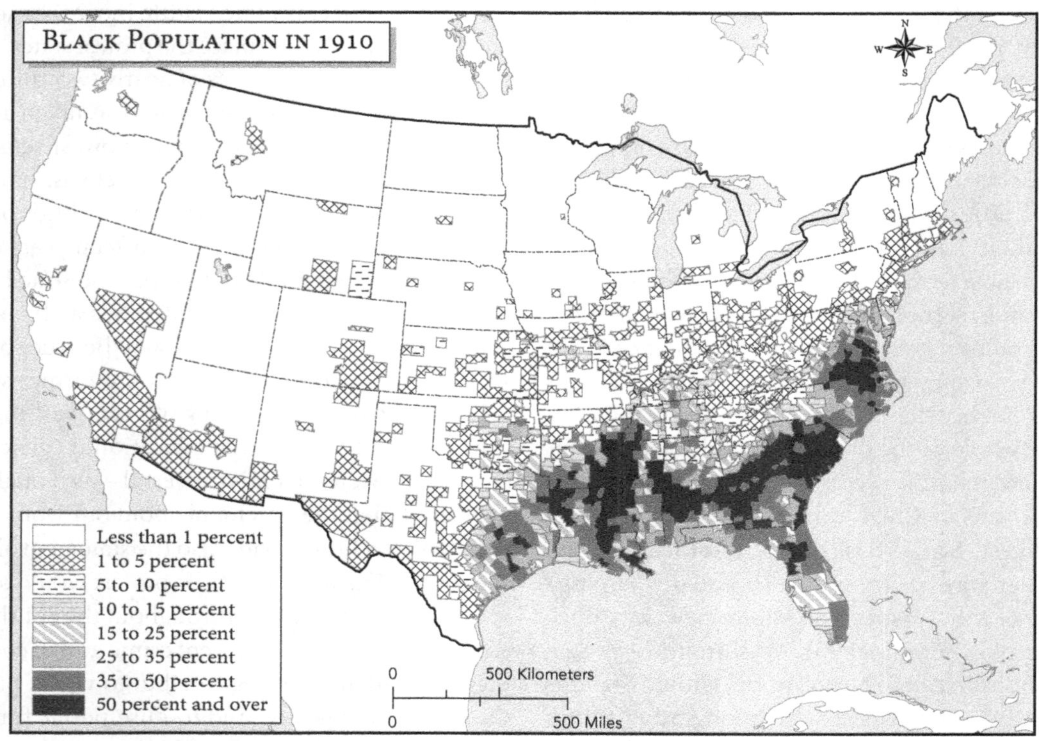

MAP 1 PERCENTAGE OF AFRICAN AMERICANS BY COUNTIES IN 1910

people friendly to his aspirations. If Mr. Washington can encourage the growth of such a feeling in the South, he will have done a good work even though he should fall short in other respects.

I think the reason first given by me is sufficient for my declining to sign the protest. The other reasons I think will justify me in feeling that I have not failed in my duty in so declining. It would be a lamentable thing to believe that all the money and all the effort on the part of the colored people since the war had not resulted in improving their condition; and if it is improving, it is on the way to favorable resolution. There are many things yet to be done; some of them, of which Mr. Washington has fought shy, the NAACP seeks to accomplish. There is plenty of room and plenty of work for both. I make no criticism of any of the gentlemen who have signed the appeal, but personally I should not, as I say, like to "pitch into" Mr. Washington.

With sincere regards and best wishes,

Charles W. Chesnutt

DRAWING CONCLUSIONS:

1. Can you put into your own words what Terrell says Frederick Douglass thinks is the appropriate way to measure progress? Can you identify what Chesnutt thinks about progress? Do you agree with either one? What other ways should we measure progress?
2. What does Chesnutt mean when he says Washington is a "professional optimist"? Can you find passages from Washington that apply to that label?
3. Identify and evaluate the strongest and weakest arguments from both Washington and Du Bois.
4. What are Chesnutt's most convincing reasons to refuse Du Bois? What are his least?
5. After reading all three documents by Washington, Du Bois, and Chesnutt, consider what you would have done if you had lived in 1910. Would you have signed Du Bois's *Appeal*? Why or why not?
6. Draw on these four authors and synthesize their arguments about progress, or the lack of progress, in the early twentieth century.

DATA ON BLACK LIFE

This section contains quantitative data about various aspects of black life in the early twentieth century. This information can be useful in many ways. You could check the claims made by many of the document authors, black and white, against the reality. You could also draw conclusions from the charts about change over time. Overall, were African Americans making progress in these decades?

GUIDING QUESTIONS:

1. Do you expect to see an overall increase, a decrease, or no change in the health, wealth, and education of African Americans over time?
2. What parts of the country do you predict will be the most positive climate for African Americans?
3. Have you ever been involved in a fundraiser? How much work was involved? How much work do you think it took to raise money for a new church building?

2.1 BLACK FARM OWNERS BY DIVISIONS, 1900–1910

This report from the Department of Commerce divided the nation into geographic divisions, listed here, and compared the number of black farm owners in 1900 and 1910. Land ownership was one of the great dreams of people emancipated by the Civil War, and it continued to be a goal for many agricultural people in the early twentieth century.

GEOGRAPHIC DIVISIONS

New England = Maine, New Hampshire, Vermont, Massachusetts, Rhode Island, Connecticut

Middle Atlantic = New York, New Jersey, Pennsylvania

East North Central = Ohio, Indiana, Illinois, Michigan, Wisconsin

West North Central = Minnesota, Iowa, Missouri, North Dakota, South Dakota, Nebraska, Kansas

South Atlantic = Delaware, Maryland, DC, Virginia, West Virginia, North Carolina, South Carolina, Georgia, Florida

East South Central = Kentucky, Tennessee, Alabama, Mississippi

West South Central = Arkansas, Louisiana, Oklahoma, Texas

Mountain = Montana, Idaho, Wyoming, Colorado, New Mexico, Arizona, Utah, Nevada

Pacific = Washington, Oregon, California

TABLE 1 BLACK FARM OWNERS BY DIVISIONS, 1900–1910

Division	1900 Owners	1910 Owners	Total Increase	Percent Increase
New England	197	240	46	+17.4%
Middle Atlantic	953	793	–160	–16.8%
East North Central	3,064	3,095	31	+ 1%
West North Central	3,908	3,379	–538	–13.8%
South Atlantic	84,389	101,135	16,746	+19.8%
East South Central	49,888	58,610	8,722	+17.5
West South Central	45,141	51,342	6,201	+13.7
Mountain	104	176	72	+69.2%
Pacific	153	211	58	37.9

2.2 BLACK HOMES (NON-FARM) OWNED IN SOUTHERN STATES, 1900–1910

This report from the Department of Commerce compares the number of black-owned homes in the south that were not farms from 1900 to 1910. The entire country in this time period experienced rising urbanization.

TABLE 2 BLACK HOMES (NON-FARM) OWNED IN SOUTHERN STATES, 1900–1910

Division	1900	1910	Total Increase	Percent Increase
South Atlantic	73,586	106,211	32,625	44.3
East South Central	40,692	60,264	19,572	48.1
West South Central	31,201	51,467	20,266	65.0

2.3 BLACK RELIGIOUS BODIES, 1890–1906

Before the Civil War, many southern states forbade or heavily policed independent religious worship practices of enslaved people. After emancipation, freed people reveled in the liberty to embrace their own religious beliefs. Even though sharecroppers earned very little profits, they donated their hard-earned money to build churches. This report from the Department of Commerce details the changes in black religious organizations from 1890 to 1906.

TABLE 3 BLACK RELIGIOUS BODIES

Category	1890	1906	Total Increase	Percent Increase
Organizations	23,462	36,770	13,308	56.7
Communicants or members	2,673,977	3,685,097	1,011,120	37.8
Places of worship: Church edifices	23,770	35,160	11,390	47.9
Value of church edifices	$26,626,448	$56,636,159	$30,009,711	112.7
Black population	7,488,676	9,446,189	1,957,513	26.1

2.4 LITERACY RATES

Both Booker T. Washington and W. E. B. DuBois discuss literacy rates in their pieces. The following chart comes from data collected by the federal government for the Census. Census takers go to houses and ask people multiple questions, including whether they can read or write. Education was a source of great controversy in American history. During the antebellum period, it was illegal to teach slaves to read and write. After emancipation, freedmen flocked to schools eager to gain knowledge. But white supremacists continued to oppose educational access for African Americans. In the Progressive Era, these two forces continued to clash.

TABLE 4 PERCENTAGE OF PERSONS FOURTEEN YEARS OLD AND OLDER WHO WERE ILLITERATE (UNABLE TO READ OR WRITE IN ANY LANGUAGE), BY RACE AND NATIVITY: 1870 TO 1920

Year	Total	White Total	White (Native Born)	White (Foreign Born)	Black and Other
1870	20.0	11.5	—	—	79.9
1880	17.0	9.4	8.7	12.0	70.0
1890	13.3	7.7	6.2	13.1	56.8
1900	10.7	6.2	4.6	12.9	44.5
1910	7.7	5.0	3.0	12.7	30.5
1920	6.0	4.0	2.0	13.1	23.0

2.5 SCHOOL ATTENDANCE RATES IN THE SOUTH

Southern schools segregated pupils by race and spent far fewer dollars per pupil in African American schools during the Jim Crow era. The following chart shows attendance rates for southern schools broken down into black, white, male, and female by age groups, but it does not specify the quality of the schools.

TABLE 5 SCHOOL ATTENDANCE RATES IN THE SOUTH

	Age 5–9	Age 10–14	Age 15–20	Age 5–20
Black Males				
1890	22.4%	48.6%	17.1%	29.5%
1900	21.6%	49.7%	14.9%	28.5%
1910	38.5%	63.7%	23.7%	41.8%
1920	50.8%	75.8%	26.8%	51.6%
Black Females				
1890	23.2%	53.1%	18.4%	31.1%
1900	22.6%	56.2%	19.7%	31.9%
1910	40.6%	70.0%	29.2%	45.6%
1920	52.3%	79.4%	31.5%	53.7%
White Males				
1890	38.4%	79.4%	33.9%	49.6%
1900	35.0%	74.3%	32.0%	46.4%
1910	52.5%	84.8%	40.6%	58.5%
1920	61.3%	89.8%	37.2%	62.8%
White Females				
1890	38.4%	76.6%	30.1%	47.6%
1900	35.0%	77.3%	31.5%	47.0%
1910	51.9%	85.8%	39.2%	57.8%
1920	61.4%	89.9%	42.0%	63.2%

2.6 LIFE EXPECTANCY AT BIRTH, FOR SELECTED THREE-YEAR AVERAGES

Many factors determine life expectancy, including nutrition, access to health care, working conditions, community status, and many intangible influences. One of the horrors of institutionalized racism was the way it cut short black lives. These charts from the Department of Commerce break down life expectancy by race and sex in the early twentieth century.

TABLE 6A LIFE EXPECTANCY AT BIRTH, FOR SELECTED THREE-YEAR AVERAGES, MALE

Year Range for Average	Black and Other Races	White	Differences in Years
1900–1902	32.5	48.2	–15.7
1909–1911	34.1	50.2	–16.1
1919–1921	47.1	56.3	-9.2

TABLE 6B LIFE EXPECTANCY AT BIRTH, FOR SELECTED THREE-YEAR AVERAGES, FEMALE

Year Range for Average	Black and Other Races	White	Differences in Years
1900–1902	35.0	51.1	–16.1
1909–1911	37.7	53.6	–15.9
1919–1921	46.9	58.5	–11.6

2.7 BLACK PERSONS EMPLOYED IN SELECTED PROFESSIONAL OCCUPATIONS FOR SELECTED YEARS

Before the Civil War there was a free black population in the North and pockets of the South where some people were able to pursue professional occupations. However, in most of the slave states the white population limited the education and job possibilities of black workers to agricultural, domestic, or artisanal occupations. With freedom from slavery came the possibility of pursuing new job dreams. This government chart shows the numbers of black professional workers in 1890 and 1910.

TABLE 7 BLACK PERSONS EMPLOYED IN SELECTED PROFESSIONAL OCCUPATIONS FOR SELECTED YEARS

Year	Teachers, Except College	Clergy	Physicians and Surgeons	Lawyers and Judges
1890	15,100	12,159	909	431
1910	29,432	17,495	3,077	798

2.8 NUMBER OF BLACK BUSINESSES FOR SELECTED YEARS

TABLE 8 NUMBER OF BLACK BUSINESSES FOR SELECTED YEARS

Year	Black Businesses	Percent Change from Previous Date
1883	10,000	150
1893	17,000	70
1903	25,000	47
1913	40,000	60

2.9 NUMBER OF AFRICAN AMERICAN MEMBERS IN CONGRESS

TABLE 9 NUMBER OF AFRICAN AMERICAN MEMBERS IN CONGRESS

Congress	Representatives	Senate	Total Voting Members
1869–1871	2	1	3
1871–1873	5	0	5
1873–1875	7	0	7
1875–1877	7	1	8
1877–1879	3	1	4
1879–1881	0	1	1
1883–1885	2	0	2
1885–1887	2	0	2
1887–1889	0	0	0
1889–1891	3	0	3
1891–1893	1	0	1
1893–1895	1	0	1
1895–1897	1	0	1
1897–1899	1	0	1
1899–1901	1	0	1
1901–1903	0	0	0*

* The number of black representatives remained at 0 until 1929.

DRAWING CONCLUSIONS:

1. What areas of the country had the greatest gains and losses? Can you try to explain why?
2. Look back at Mary Church Terrell's discussion of the importance of the home. Analyze how the increase in home ownership speaks to her values.
3. In addition to a religious worship space, what other functions might a church building be used for in an African American community?
4. Compare literacy rates to Du Bois and Washington's assertions about educational levels. Which one had a more accurate assessment?
5. What happens to school attendance after age fifteen? What could be the reasons for this trend?
6. Overall, do these statistics suggest this is an age of progress for African Americans?

EDUCATION

These documents contain a sharp exchange between the white supremacist Thomas Dixon, Jr. and the black math professor Kelly Miller. Before emancipation, most slave states forbid teaching slaves to read or learn other skills. Slave owners considered it dangerous, since educated slaves could learn to run away or organize a rebellion. White southerners continued to argue against black education after emancipation well into the twentieth century.

GUIDING QUESTION:

In the following documents, consider both the white southern attitude and the black activist response. Additionally, look at images of African American students from the time period and check back to the data section for numbers on literacy and school attendance. What do the following documents reveal about education and progress in this time period?

3.1 THOMAS DIXON, JR. ON EDUCATION

Dixon was a Baptist minister from North Carolina who attended Johns Hopkins, where he befriended future president Woodrow Wilson. He moved to New York City and became a bestselling author with a trilogy of novels on the south with viciously racist depictions of African Americans. The second novel in the series, *The Clansman*, portrayed the post–Civil War Ku Klux Klan as a heroic organization, ultimately inspiring white southerners to reform the group in 1915. The following excerpt is from the first novel in the series, *The Leopard's Spots: A Romance of the White Man's Burden, 1865–1900* and gives a glimpse into Dixon's thinking about racial difference. In this scenario Gaston, a white scalawag, has proposed a system of industrial education to a Preacher. This is the Preacher's response.

"The more you educate, the more impossible you make his [the African American's] position in a democracy. Education! Can you change the color of the Negro's skin, the kink of his hair, the bulge of his lip, or the beat of his heart, with a spelling book or a machine? The Negro is the human donkey. You can train him, but you can't make of him a horse. Mate him with a horse, you lose the horse, and get a larger donkey called a mule, incapable of preserving his species. What is called our race prejudice is simply God's first law of nature—the instinct of self-preservation."

DRAWING CONCLUSIONS:

1. What does Dixon think about the potential for African Americans to be educated?
2. Explain his reference to horses and donkeys. What parallel is he drawing with humans?
3. How might this mindset be used to justify segregation?

From Thomas Dixon, Jr., *The Leopard's Spots: A Romance of the White Man's Burden—1865–1900* (New York: Doubleday and Page, 1902), 460.

3.2 KELLY MILLER CRITICIZES THOMAS DIXON, JR.

Kelly Miller was an African American scholar and an activist. He taught mathematics at Howard University in Washington, DC. In this piece, he responds to Dixon's novel *The Leopard's Spots*.

You ask: "Can you change the color of the Negro's skin, the kind of his hair, the bulge of his lip, or the beat of his heart, with a spelling book or a machine?" This rhetorical outburst does great credit to your literary skill, and is calculated to delight the simple; but analysis fails to reveal in it any pregnant meaning. Since civilization is not an attribute of the color of skin, or curl of hair or curve of lip, there is no necessity for changing such physical peculiarities, and if there was, the spelling book and the machine would be very unlikely instruments for its accomplishment. But why, may I ask, would you desire to change the Negro's heart throb, which already beats at a normal human pace?

The solution of the race problem in America is indeed a grave and serious matter. . . . The whole spirit of your propaganda is to add to its intensity and aggravation. You stir the slumbering fires of race wrath into an uncontrollable flame. . . . Your teachings subvert the foundations of law and established order. You are the high priest of lawlessness, the prophet of anarchy. . . . You openly urge your fellow citizens to override all law, human and divine. Are you aware of the force and effect of these words? "Could fatuity reach a sublimer height than the idea that the white man will stand idly by and see the performance? What will he do when put to the test? He will do exactly what his white neighbor in the North does when Negro threatens his bread-kill him!" These words breath out hatred and slaughter and suggest the murder of innocent men whose only crime is quest for the God-given right to work. You poison the mind and pollute the imagination through the subtle influence of letters. . . . The soul of the mob is stirred by suggestion of hatred and slaughter, as a famished beast at the smell of blood . . . To wantonly stir up the fires of race antipathy is as execrable a deed as flaunting a red rag in the face of a bull at summer's picnic, or raising a false cry of "fire" in a crowded house. Human society could not exist one hour except on the basis of law which holds the baser passions of men in restraint.

DRAWING CONCLUSIONS:

1. What criticisms does Miller have of Dixon?
2. Evaluate Miller's claim that Dixon's novel could increase violence in real life.
3. What do you think is the relationship between art and real life? Why does fiction matter?

From Miller, Kelly, Daniel Murray Pamphlet Collection, and African American Pamphlet Collection. As to the leopard's spots: an open letter to Thomas Dixon, Jr. Washington, D.C.: Published by Kelly Miller, Howard University: Hayworth Publishing House, 1905. Pdf. https://www.loc.gov/item/05033680/.

3.3 "A NEGRO STUDENT AT HAMPTON"

After the Civil War, northern abolitionists wanted to ensure that formerly enslaved people could become educated and successful and supported schools for this purpose. One of these abolitionists, General Samuel Chapman Armstrong, founded Hampton Institute in Washington, DC. The mission of the school was to educate people to become teachers, in the hopes of spreading education even more broadly. Within that mission was an emphasis on job training skills, such as carpentry, masonry, and other skilled trades. The following image shows a student at Hampton Institute.

GUIDING QUESTIONS:

1. Have you ever taken a selfie in your dorm room? If so, what did you want to convey about yourself? For example, did you want people to think you were fun? smart? sexy? cool? Think about how you conveyed that message with your image. How did you dress? Pose? What did your room look like?
2. Keeping your own presentation of self in mind, turn that lens onto the following image. What are the student and photographer trying to convey with this century-old selfie?

FIGURE 1 CADET STUDYING

Source: Schomburg Center for Research in Black Culture, Jean Blackwell Hutson Research and Reference Division, The New York Public Library. "A Negro student in his room at Hampton." The New York Public Library Digital Collections. 1910. http://digitalcollections.nypl.org/items/510d47df-8d73-a3d9-e040-e00a18064a99

DRAWING CONCLUSIONS:

1. How is the student dressed? What is he doing? What is the condition of his room?
2. What message does he convey about himself?
3. If you read the beginning Case Study and the Dixon document, you'll know that the education of African Americans was controversial. How could this picture be an argument in favor of African American education?
4. When you take a selfie at college, do you feel the burden of proving your right to an education?

3.4 SCHOOL CHILDREN IN THE SOUTH

This image from the Library of Congress's collection is not entirely identified. It was taken between 1900 and 1910, and based on the foliage, it is definitely in the South, most likely South Carolina.

GUIDING QUESTIONS:

1. We do not know much about the people in this picture, so we have to rely on inference. What can you glean about the teacher and students?
2. What message does the photographer and subjects want the viewer to get?

FIGURE 2 SCHOOL CHILDREN IN THE SOUTH

LC-DIG-ppmsca-13304 (digital file from original photograph) LC-USZ62-26381 (b&w film copy neg.) Library of Congress Prints and Photographs Division Washington, D.C. 20540 USA

DRAWING CONCLUSIONS:

1. Does the school building look well-maintained?
2. Does it look like the teacher and students dressed up for the picture? Did they coordinate their outfits? What does that tell you about what image they want to project?
3. If you were a black parent in the South during the Progressive Era, would you want to send your child to this school? Why or why not?

3.5 MARY MCLEOD BETHUNE STARTS A SCHOOL

Mary McLeod Bethune was an educator in Florida. She started the Bethune Institute, which later became Bethune-Cookman College. Here she describes her inspiration and vision to start her school.

While at Haines Institute, I had occasion to pay a visit to Tuskegee Institute and there I saw for the first time the great institution built by that great architect of the lives of many Negro youths, Booker Washington.

I went through Mr. Washington's Institution [Tuskegee Institute] and studied it, making mental tabulations as I noticed certain aspects. I talked with Booker Washington. After I had seen this marvelous institution in all of its significancy, I began to think. A great realization dawned upon me. I was electrified with a resolution to do on a slightly different scale and in a different manner, perhaps, what Mr. Washington had in mind and what he had already started out to do. The thought thrilled me as the seeds of Bethune Cookman College stated through a process of fertilization in my mind. Conception was taking place as I becam[e] impregnated with a desire that has become my life's work and achievement. I turned over ideas in my mind slowly, meditatively, and fondly. I began to nurture what had been conceived.

I envisioned an institution in which would be taught the essentials of home making, of the skilled trades, but there would also be courses stressing the importance of citizenship and the duty of the citizen using his voting power. These courses, I felt must be unduly stressed, as a measure of realizing citizenship in its entirety. At the head of this institution would be a woman who would preside—a "modern matriarch, head of the family." That was my dream in its conception and period of restraint or confinement. It became fixed in my very being and I knew that the birth of the institution of my mind and dream lay in the offing. . . .

While at Palatka, I heard of horrible social conditions existing among the Negroes of Daytona Beach, Florida. I set out on a tour of investigation. I sensed in Daytona Beach the chance for which I longed. Here was the chance to realize an absorbing longing. My nurtured dream was crying for birth and I was determined that it should be born in this place of enormous ignorance and the most limited educational facilities, violence, crime and lack of opportunity. Here my institution could fill a great need. Here I would build my dream.

When I arrived in Daytona Beach, I had one dollar and a half in actual money. No place for shelter, and certainly no funds for my proposed institution for girls. A man rented me a little cottage with the promise from me that he should be paid within a limited time. I secured boxes from the various stores in my neighborhood and used them for chairs, while one box served for a desk. Several persons who were in accord with and caught the spirit of my endeavor gave me a bed or two and bits of discarded matting and carpet.

From Spruill, Marjorie J., and Carol Bleser. *Southern Women in the Progressive Era: A Reader*. Univ of South Carolina Press, 2019.

I worked arduously in the little cottage in an attempt to make it livable. All of my efforts were made in good faith that I might be able to yet realize my dream. By October 4, 1904, my little building was ready. There was much crudity about it, but I had worked and cleaned it thoroughly. It was on this day that the Daytona Educational and Industrial Training School opened its doors, and five little girls entered. . . .

A few months later that organization was made permanent, a charter was secured and the Daytona Industrial and Educational Training School was made much more secure. Tears welled within me and a great happiness flooded me as sufficient funds were obtained to enable some of my ideals to be realized. The birth of my dream was realized. I needed only nurse and rear it to a rich useful maturity. That, I was confident I could do, for such was the dictates of my innermost self.

DRAWING CONCLUSIONS:

1. Compare Bethune's educational goals with the educational goals of your school.
2. What does this account tell us about southern conditions?

3.6 BETHUNE WITH A LINE OF GIRLS

This image shows Mary McLeod Bethune with students from the school she started.

FIGURE 3 MARY MCLEOD BETHUNE WITH A LINE OF GIRLS FROM THE SCHOOL

Source: Mary McLeod Bethune with a line of girls from the school. ca 1905. Black & white photonegative, 4 x 5 in. State Archives of Florida, Florida Memory. https://www.floridamemory.com/items/show/149519, accessed 7 February 2020.

DRAWING CONCLUSIONS:

1. What values are conveyed by this image? Consider many factors, including how people are dressed and how they are posed. Even look at their feet!
2. Would it be appropriate to call Mary McLeod Bethune a progressive?

3.7 W. E. B. DU BOIS ON A UNIVERSITY EDUCATION

See section 1.3 for information on Du Bois. This excerpt, from *Souls of Black Folk*, gives us a window into what Du Bois considered to be the purpose of a college education. Atlanta University, where Du Bois worked as a scholar and teacher for several years, is one of many Historically Black Colleges in the United States. During this time period, Booker T. Washington was extremely successful in raising money from white people for his school, Tuskegee Institute. Many white people thought industrial education, education for specific jobs, was the best and maybe only type of education black children should receive. Here Du Bois makes a case for a different kind of education.

The hundred hills of Atlanta are not all crowned with factories. On one, toward the west, the setting sun throws three buildings in bold relief against the sky. The beauty of the group lies in its simple unity:—a broad lawn of green rising from the red street and mingled roses and peaches; north and south, two plain and stately halls; and in the midst, half hidden in ivy, a larger building, boldly graceful, sparingly decorated, and with one low spire. It is a restful group,—one never looks for more; it is all here, all intelligible. There I live, and there I hear from day to day the low hum of restful life. In winter's twilight, when the red sun glows, I can see the dark figures pass between the halls to the music of the night-bell. In the morning, when the sun is golden, the clang of the day-bell brings the hurry and laughter of three hundred young hearts from hall and street, and from the busy city below,—children all dark and heavy-haired,—to join their clear young voices in the music of the morning sacrifice. In a half-dozen class-rooms they gather then,—here to follow the love-song of Dido, here to listen to the tale of Troy divine; there to wander among the stars, there to wander among men and nations,—and elsewhere other well-worn ways of knowing this queer world. Nothing new, no time-saving devices,—simply old time-glorified methods of delving for Truth, and searching out the hidden beauties of life, and learning the good of living. The riddle of existence is the college curriculum that was laid before the Pharaohs, that was taught in the groves by Plato, that formed the trivium and quadrivium, and is to-day laid before the freedmen's sons by Atlanta University. And this course of study will not change; its methods will grow more deft and effectual, its content richer by toil of scholar and sight of seer; but the true college will ever have one goal,—not to earn meat, but to know the end and aim of that life which meat nourishes.

DRAWING CONCLUSIONS:

1. DuBois uses many lyrical phrases in the first half of this excerpt to describe his school. What is the effect of this wording? How does he want the reader to feel about this place?
2. Put into your own words what kind of classes students are taking.
3. Put into your own words what DuBois is saying should be the goal of a college. Compare this goal with current-day goals of college. Are there still debates on whether college should prepare students to "earn meat" or encourage them to be "delving for Truth?"

From W. E. B. Du Bois, *Souls of Black Folk*, ed. David Blight and Robert Gooding-Williams (Bedford: St. Martin's, 1997), 87.

WORK

The following documents demonstrate tensions between white and black workers in the early twentieth century. In the post–Civil War era, the Knights of Labor (KOL) became the largest union in the nation. The KOL was very inclusive, welcoming all races, ethnicities, and skill levels. After a number of violent labor upheavals, businesses demonized the KOL as radicals and the union disintegrated. The American Federation of Labor (AFL) rose to power by tacking to the middle. This union emphasized "bread and butter" issues such as higher pay and only let in skilled laborers to increase their bargaining power with businesses.

Many people who identified with the Progressive movement sympathized with the plight of workers and supported the expansion of unions to support workers' attempts to better their wages and working conditions. If an occupation could get enough workers to join their union, they had a large force to bring to the bargaining table. If bargaining broke down, one of the last resorts of a union was to strike. A strike is when workers stopped working to force the bosses to realize the importance of workers and come back to the bargaining table. Often in a strike workers would picket in front of the factory or shop to publicize their activism and prevent new people from being hired. One of the greatest threats to a strike was strike-breakers, also called "scabs." Strike breakers were non-union members who crossed the picket line and took the old jobs at the wages and working conditions set by management. Too many strikebreakers could destroy a union.

Unionization depends on the willingness of workers to bond with one another over their shared condition and work collectively to bargain with their employer. You can see from these documents how union members addressed one another as "brother" and "sister," indicating their attachment to the idea of a union as family. However, many white workers could not envision reaching out across racial and ethnic lines to expand their working family. Read the following documents and consider what tensions surrounded work and unions, and what bearing they had on the big question.

GUIDING QUESTIONS:

1. If gains for workers won by labor unions were part of the Progressive Era, did African Americans share in those successes?
2. What reasons do you think white union members would have for being hostile to black workers?
3. Part of the dream of union organizers is to foster a sense of unity among workers. Karl Marx called this class consciousness. America is unique among industrial nations for having less unity among workers. What divisions do you see among workers in these documents?

4.1 THE AFL ACCUSES BLACK WORKERS OF BEING "CHEAP MEN" IN THE *AMERICAN FEDERATIONIST*, 1901

This excerpt from the magazine for the American Federation of Labor (AFL) exposes the attitude of union members to black workers.

The real difficulty in the matter is that the colored workers have allowed themselves to be used with too frequent telling effect by their employers as to injure the cause and interests of themselves as well as of the white workers. They have too often allowed themselves to be regarded as "cheap men," and all realize that "cheap men" are not only an impediment to the attainment of the workers' just rights, and the progress of civilization, but will tie themselves to the slough of despond and despair. The antipathy that we know some union workers have against the colored man is not because of his color, but because of the fact that generally he is a "cheap man." It is the constant aim of our movement to relieve all workers, white and black, from such an unenviable and unprofitable condition.

From "Trade Union Attitude Toward Colored Workers," *American Federationist* (April 1901) In *Black Workers: A Documentary History from Colonial Tmes to the Present*, ed. Philip S. Foner and Ronald L. Lewis, (Philadelphia: Temple University Press, 1989), 241–244.

4.2 "THE NEGRO AND THE LABOR UNIONS" BY BOOKER T. WASHINGTON FROM THE *ATLANTIC MONTHLY*, 1913

For background on Booker T. Washington, see 1.2. In this article, Washington explains why black workers avoid unions and why white workers resent black workers.

Another thing which is to some extent peculiar about the Negro in the Southern states, is that the average Negro is more accustomed to work for persons than for wages. When he gets a job, therefore, he is inclined to consider the source from which it comes. The Negro is himself a friendly sort of person, and it makes a great deal of difference to him whether he believes the man he is working for is his friend or his enemy. One reason for this is that he has found in the past that the friendship and confidence of a good white man, who stands well in the community, are a valuable asset in time of trouble. For this reason he does not always understand, and does not like, an organization which seems to be founded on a sort of impersonal enmity to the man by whom he is employed; just as in the Civil War all the people in the North were the enemies of all the people in the South, even when the man on the one side was the brother of the man on the other.

I have tried to suggest in what I have said why it is true, as it seems to me, that the Negro is naturally not inclined toward labor unions. But aside from this natural disposition of the Negro there is unquestionably a very wide-spread prejudice and distrust of labor unions among Negroes generally.

One does not have to go far to discover the reason for this. In several instances Negroes are expressly excluded from membership in the unions. In other cases individual Negroes have been refused admittance to unions where no such restrictions existed, and have been in consequence shut out from employment at their trades.

For this and other reasons, Negroes, who have been shut out, or believed they had been shut out, of employment by the unions, have been in the past very willing strike-breakers. It is another illustration of the way in which prejudice works, also, that the strikers seemed to consider it a much greater crime for a Negro, who had been denied an opportunity to work at his trade, to take the place of a striking employee than it was for a white man to do the same thing. Not only have Negro strikebreakers been savagely beaten and even murdered by strikers or their sympathizers, but in some instances every Negro, no matter what his occupation, who lived in the vicinity of the strike has found himself in danger.

Originally published in the *Atlantic Monthly* 101 (June 1913). In *Black Workers: A Documentary History from Colonial Tmes to the Present*, ed. Philip S. Foner and Ronald L. Lewis, (Philadelphia: Temple University Press, 1989), 285–301.

4.3 GEORGE H. PETERS, UNION FIREMAN, WRITES TO THE *LOCOMOTIVE FIREMEN'S MAGAZINE*, 1902

Trains ran on energy produced by burning coal to create steam. The men who worked on this dirty and dangerous job successfully organized into a national union called the Locomotive Firemen. Traditionally they only had white members. In 1902, their magazine published an article questioning whether the union should welcome black firemen. Letters poured in from around the country on both sides of the issue. This one is from a fireman in New York city.

I think we can make a big improvement in the Negro by taking him into our labor organizations for, as he is, there is no ambition in him; he lacks the vital force of dissatisfaction. So let us teach him what our great organizations are for—then you will see a big improvement in his economic condition as well as that of the South. I think this will help to solve the labor problem in the South. The Negro will accept his inferiority to the white man at all times. So let us go on with whatever we have to do that means universal good, fear nothing, ignore all obstacles, and throw ourselves into the effort, and know that we are setting electric forces into action which shall surely some time bring in the results which we desire. No great worthy purpose is ever lost.

From George H. Peters, "Letter to *Locomotive Firemen's Magazine*" (August 1902). In *Black Workers: A Documentary History from Colonial Tmes to the Present*, ed. Philip S. Foner and Ronald L. Lewis, (Philadelphia: Temple University Press, 1989), 254.

4.4 UNNAMED UNION FIREMAN FROM LOUISIANA WRITES TO THE *LOCOMOTIVE FIREMEN'S MAGAZINE*, 1902

The next month after George H. Peters's letter a union member from Louisiana sent in a rebuttal attacking his position.

The negro can organize on his own responsibility if he likes, but he can never affiliate with southern organizations of any kind. The firemen of the South have yet a great work to do among themselves, without crossing the color line and reaching out after Mr. "Burr head," to assist him to a place of safety and security, protected by the mantle the Locomotive Firemen now wear with pride, bought with a great price. What has the negro done to merit recognition by the Firemen? The brother from New York says the negro will accept his inferiority to the white man at all times. Perhaps this is so where he lives, but all southern men would laugh at the brother's ignorance of the negro, as we find him in the South, for if he is given a foot, he tries to take a block. In many, many cases, he is thick headed and non-progressive, and when he goes to school a couple of years he begins to think he knows it all, and it only makes a worthless fool of him. The southern man has done far more to advance and uplight the negro than he is given credit for, but we draw the line when it comes to taking him into our worthy order.

"Member of 522" of Shreveport, LA, "Letter to *Locomotive Firemen's Magazine,*" September 1902, in *Black Workers: A Documentary History from Colonial Tmes to the Present*, ed. Philip S. Foner and Ronald L. Lewis, (Philadelphia: Temple University Press, 1989), 255.

4.5 UPTON SINCLAIR'S *THE JUNGLE*

Upton Sinclair became famous for his novel *The Jungle*, which follows the journey of an immigrant man, Jurgis, who seeks work to support his family in the meat-packing district of Chicago. Sinclair hoped to impress his readers with the injustices of unskilled laborers who had to navigate a brutal world of unsafe working conditions and low pay. But audiences paid more attention to the unsanitary conditions of meat preparations. In other words, they were grossed out. The novel made a huge impact on Americans, who pressured the government to take action on food safety. Less noticed are the brief instances of casual racism in the novel. The following excerpt shows Jurgis during a strike. A strike is when workers collectively decide to stop work in order to bargain for better benefits, such as higher pay or safer working conditions. Jurgis has become a scab, someone who works while others are striking. He observes other strikebreakers, particularly immigrants and African Americans brought in by the company to undermine the strength of the union.

For the present, his [Jurgis's] work being over, he was free to ride into the city, by a railroad direct from the yards, or else to spend the night in a room where cots had been laid in rows. He chose the latter, but to his regret, for all night long gangs of strikebreakers kept arriving. As very few of the better class of workingmen could be got for such work, these specimens of the new American hero [a scab] contained an assortment of the criminals and thugs of the city, besides Negroes and the lowest foreigners—Greeks, Roumanians, Sicilians, and Slovaks. They had been attracted more by the prospect of disorder than by the big wages; and they made the night hideous with singing and carousing, and only went to sleep when the time came for them to get up to work.

In the morning before Jurgis had finished his breakfast, "Pat" Murphy ordered him to one of the superintendents, who questioned him as to his experience in the work of the killing room. His heart began to thump with excitement, for he divined instantly that his hour had come—that he was to be a boss!

Some of the foremen were union members, and many who were not had gone out with the men. It was in the killing department that the packers had been left most in the lurch, and precisely here that they could least afford it; the smoking and canning and salting of meat might wait, and all the by-products might be wasted—but fresh meats must be had, or the restaurants and hotels and brownstone houses would feel the pinch, and then "public opinion" would take a startling turn.

An opportunity such as this would not come twice to a man; and Jurgis seized it. Yes, he knew the work, the whole of it, and he could teach it to others. But if he took the job and gave satisfaction he would expect to keep it—they would not turn him off at the end of the strike? To which the superintendent replied that he might safely trust Durham's for that—they proposed to teach these unions a lesson, and most of all those foremen who had gone back on them. Jurgis would receive five dollars a day during the strike, and twenty-five a week after it was settled.

From Upton Sinclair, *The Jungle*, chapter 26, https://www.gutenberg.org/files/140/140-h/140-h.htm

So our friend got a pair of "slaughter pen" boots and "jeans," and flung himself at his task. It was a weird sight, there on the killing beds—a throng of stupid black Negroes, and foreigners who could not understand a word that was said to them, mixed with pale-faced, hollow-chested bookkeepers and clerks, half-fainting for the tropical heat and the sickening stench of fresh blood—and all struggling to dress a dozen or two cattle in the same place where, twenty-four hours ago, the old killing gang had been speeding, with their marvelous precision, turning out four hundred carcasses every hour!

The Negroes and the "toughs" from the Levee did not want to work, and every few minutes some of them would feel obligated to retire and recuperate. In a couple of days Durham and Company had electric fans up to cool off the rooms for them, and even couches for them to rest on; and meantime they could go out and find a shady corner and take a "snooze," and as there was no place for any one in particular, and no system, it might be hours before their boss discovered them. As for the poor office employees, they did their best, moved to it by terror; thirty of them had been "fired" in a bunch that first morning for refusing to serve, besides a number of women clerks and typewriters who had declined to act as waitresses.

It was such a force as this that Jurgis had to organize. He did his best, flying here and there, placing them in rows and showing them the tricks; he had never given an order in his life before, but he had taken enough of them to know, and he soon fell into the spirit of it, and roared and stormed like any old stager. He had not the most tractable pupils, however. "See hyar, boss," a big black "buck" would begin, "ef you doan' like the way Ah does dis job, you kin get somebody else to do it." Then a crowd would gather and listen, muttering threats. After the first meal nearly all the steel knives had been missing, and now every Negro had one, ground to a fine point, hidden in his boots.

[after more description of the workplace, Sinclair turns to how the city changes after thousands of strikebreakers are brought by the company to live in the packing districts.]

Just at this time the mayor was boasting that he had put an end to gambling and prize fighting in the city; but here a swarm of professional gamblers had leagued themselves with the police to fleece the strikebreakers; and any night, in the big open space in front of Brown's, one might see brawny Negroes stripped to the waist and pounding each other for money, while a howling throng of three or four thousand surged about, men and women, young white girls from the country rubbing elbows with big buck Negroes with daggers in their boots, while rows of woolly heads peered down from every window of the surrounding factories. The ancestors of these black people had been savages in Africa; and since then they had been chattel slaves, or had been held down by a community ruled by the traditions of slavery. Now for the first time they were free—free to gratify every passion, free to wreck themselves. They were wanted to break a strike, and when it was broken they would be shipped away, and their present masters would never see them again; and so whisky and women were brought in by the carload and sold to them, and hell was let loose in the yards. Every night there were stabbings and shootings; it was said that the packers had blank permits, which enabled them to ship dead bodies from the city without troubling the authorities. They lodged men and women on the same floor; and with the night there began a saturnalia of debauchery—scenes such as never before had been witnessed in America. And as women were the dregs from the brothels of Chicago, and the men were for the most part ignorant country Negroes, the nameless diseases of vice were soon rife; and this where food was being handled which was sent out to every corner of the civilized world.

4.6 SAMUEL GOMPERS ON BLACK STRIKEBREAKERS

This newspaper reporter describes a 1905 speech in Minnesota, where the head of the AFL, Samuel Gompers, spoke candidly about African American workers in Chicago. The AFL allowed member unions to discriminate against African Americans and bar them from membership. Many African Americans thus did not have a feeling of solidarity with unions and were willing to break a strike.

Mr. Gompers spoke pointedly of the strike breaking in Chicago by negroes. He states that organized labor desired no controversy with the negroes; "but," he said, "if the colored man continues to lend himself to the work of tearing down what the white man has built up, a race hatred worse than any ever known before will result. Caucasian civilization will serve notice that its uplifting process is not to be interfered with in any such way."

From Green, W., McBride, J., Gompers, S., American Federation of Labor., AFL-CIO. The American federationist. Washington, D.C.,[etc.]: American Federation of Labor and Congress of Industrial Organizations [etc.].

4.7 WOMEN'S LOCAL IN THE STOCKYARDS

Mary McDowall was a wealthy white woman who worked in Chicago's settlement house and sympathized with the labor movement. Here she describes a lively exchange in a women's union meeting.

It was a dramatic occasion on that evening, when the first colored girl asked for admission. The president, an Irish girl whose father . . had left his job because a colored man had been put to work with him, was naturally expected to be prejudiced against the reception of a negro woman. Hannah, as doorkeeper, called out in her own social way, "A colored sister is at the door. What'll I do with her?" "Admit her," called back the president, "and let all of ye's give her a hearty welcome." The tall, dignified, good-looking, well-dressed colored girl, much frightened walked down the center aisle of the gymnasium, while the room rang with cheers and the clapping of hands. One felt that here was a law stronger than that of Roberts Rules of Order.

Soon after a meeting, when the question in the ritual "Have you any grievances?" was put to the house full of girls, black and white, Polish, Bohemian, Irish, Croatian, and Hungarian, a shy sensitive colored girl (morbidly sensitive black girl) arose and said, "A Polish girl was always taunting her on her color." The union demanded that the Polish and the colored stand and each give a reason for this unseemly conduct. "Well," says the Polish girl, "I did tease her, but she called me a Polock, and I won't stand that." The hearty, good-natured laugh from their fellow workers cleared the international atmosphere, and they were told to cease teasing each other. "Ain't you ashamed of yourselves,?" said the President. "You promised in the union to be sisters and here you are fighting. Now shake hands and don't bring any more of your personal grievances here. Tell it to your shop steward and remember this is where only shop grievances are to be brought."

Black Workers: A Documentary History from Colonial Tmes to the Present, ed. Philip S. Foner and Ronald L. Lewis, (Philadelphia: Temple University Press, 1989), 301–302.

4.8 MINING JOBS IN SEATTLE, WASHINGTON

In 1909, a paper in Washington State called *The Seattle Republican* published a special edition on what they called "Negro Progress" to celebrate the advancements of African American residents in Seattle and encourage more people to migrate there. This eighty-page edition contained images of beautiful homes, biographies of prosperous citizens, celebrations of black organizations, and many other testimonials to life in the city. In the following excerpt, the author, most likely the editor of the paper, makes a case to lure black workers to the area. The term "Open Shop" describes a company where the employer refuses to bargain exclusively with union workers. Unions prefer "closed shops" where all workers have to join the union and thus hold more bargaining power with the employer. In an open shop, workers can choose whether to join or not.

Open Shop—The Pacific Coast Company adopted the "open shop" policy fifteen or more years ago, when it imported some 600 Negro miners from the East to take a host of striking union miners' places in their mining camps and it has maintained the open shop policy ever since. There are at present large numbers of colored men employed by the Pacific Coast Company at their mines located at Franklin, Black Diamond, Lawson, Newcastle and other lesser mining properties, nevertheless there is ample room for many more and 300 or more colored miners would be given steady employment at those mines if they could be had. That such miners would be given a "square deal" the prospective miner is referred to George W. Johnson, John Hall, E. H. Richards, Gordon Carter, Emanuel Moore and Charley Scott, all well-known colored miners of Franklin, Wash. and Rev. S. A. Franklin, Henry Jones, of Newcastle, Wash., who have been in the employ of this company for the past sixteen years. These men have been given steady employment at good wages and not only have they, but all others who wanted. Many if not all of these men have invested their surplus earnings in real estate in and about Seattle and their holdings have quadrupled in value and they therefore have made big money both going and coming.

Good Wages—As at all of the mines in this section the men at the mines of the Pacific Coast Company are paid from $2.50 to $6 per day. Living at the mines is cheaper by far than in the city, as the industrious miner has so many opportunities to cut down his store bill by raising all the vegetables including potatoes and onions that his family can consume the year round. Not only raise his vegetables, but the enterprising miner can have his own milch cow, raise his chickens and a few pigs for good measure. The editor of *The Seattle Republican* is thoroughly conversant with the existing conditions at the mines of the Pacific Coast Company and therefore cheerfully recommends them as places where colored men may do extremely well from a financial standpoint and for Southern colored miners it would prove a most desirable change. Colored miners who desire to come to the Northwest and have not sufficient funds to bring their families along with them might come themselves and after they have given evidence of "making

From https://wshs.contentdm.oclc.org/digital/collection/digipubs/id/1463

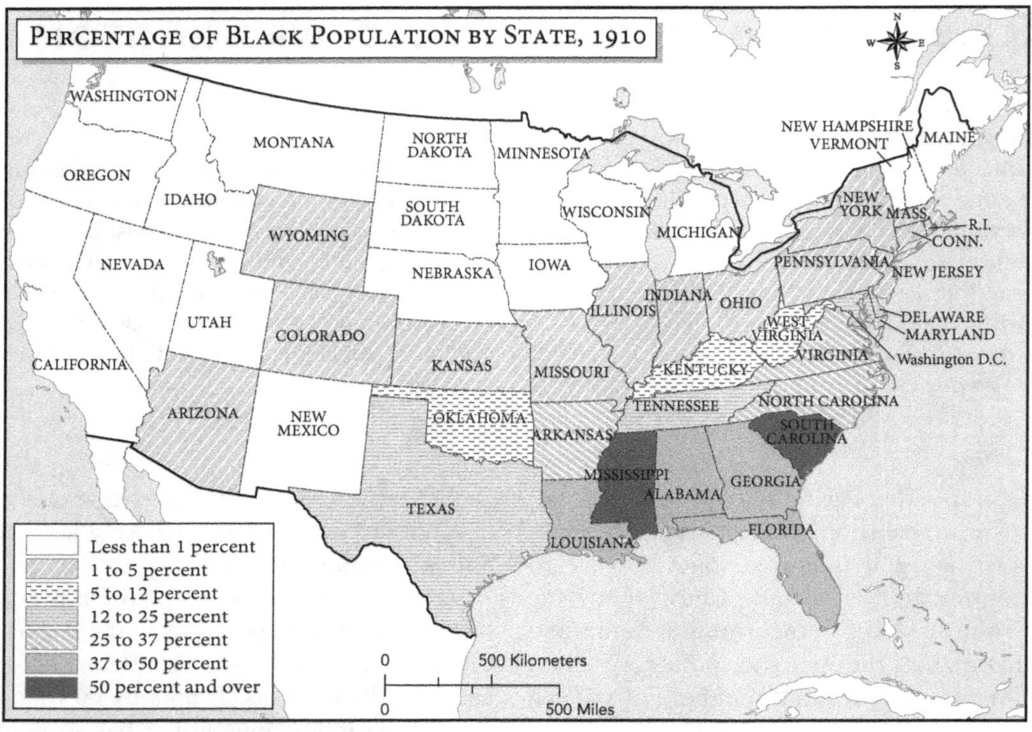

MAP 2 AFRICAN AMERICAN POPULATION IN 1910

good" the company would send railroad tickets for their families and give them credit in the store until they earned sufficient money to look out for themselves. By addressing James Anderson, superintendent of mines in the care of the Pacific Coast Company, Seattle, Washington, or either of the colored miners named above, or The Seattle Republican, Seattle, Wash., any question you might desire to have answered would be cheerfully as well as immediately done. There are good schools at all of the mines, churches, and secret societies. The company has good and commodious houses ready for occupancy and house furnishings to begin housekeeping may be had at the company's store at the most reasonable rates.

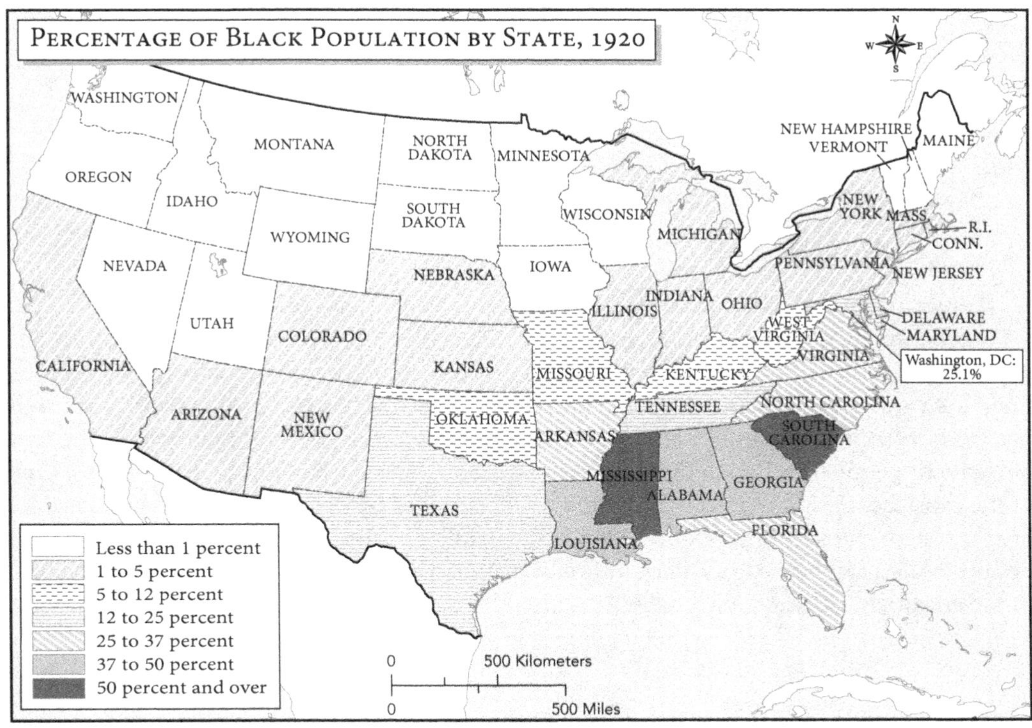

MAP 3 AFRICAN AMERICAN POPULATION IN 1920

DRAWING CONCLUSIONS:

1. What concerns do union members have about black workers? What concerns do black workers have about unions?
2. Evaluate what advantages and disadvantages black workers would consider before making the decision to move to a new state to work.
3. Compare and contrast the fictional representation of black workers in *The Jungle* with description of life in Seattle for black miners. What do they reveal about different visions of where African Americans fit into the American Dream?
4. To what extent would a black worker who moved to a job in a new state be interested in joining a union and be welcome in that union?

LYNCHING

Many African American activists highlighted the horrifying phenomenon of lynching. Lynching is a mob killing of an individual accused of a breach of law or custom. Instead of following the Constitutional rights of due process for a trial by a jury of peers, mobs drew their own conclusions without evidence and executed accused criminals. The accused had no lawyers and no ability to present evidence or call witnesses on their behalf. The vast majority of people lynched in the Progressive Era were African Americans in the South. One of the most frustrating aspects of lynching was the lack of concern from the formal criminal justice system. Most mob members who participated in these murders were never arrested or imprisoned for their crime. Black journalists and activists worked to expose the racial bias in the criminal justice system.

5.1 A JUDGE MEASURES WHITE AND BLACK LIFE

The following document, reported in *The Crisis* magazine, the journal of the NAACP, centers on a judge in Georgia who refused to prevent the lynching of two men accused of murder.

GUIDING QUESTIONS:

1. What should be the responsibility of the criminal justice system for the safety of accused criminals?
2. Should citizens be treated equally before the law regardless of race?

Public opinion in the State of Georgia seems somewhat aroused over a recent lynching and it is possible the offenders may be prosecuted. Two colored men had been arrested, Allen for an alleged attack on a white woman, and Watts for "loitering" nearby in a "suspicious manner." Judge Charles H. Brand ordered Allen brought to Monroe for trial. It was known that the citizens had organized to lynch the man and Governor Brown asked Judge Brand if he wanted troops at the trial. Judge Brand returned an evasive answer and referred the Governor to Sheriff Stark. The latter said that Judge Brand would have to ask for troops. No word came, and the man was sent to Walton County in charge of two officers. The train was stopped by a mob, Allen taken off, tied to a telegraph pole and shot, while the passengers on the train looked on.

The mob, several hundred strong, and unmasked, then marched to Monroe, about six miles away, where Joe Watts was confined in jail. They boldly proceeded to the jail, stormed it, took out the Negro, hanged him to a tree and shot him.

Both men denied that they were guilty, and there seems to have been no strong evidence against them. Members of the legislature say there will be an investigation and probably impeachment proceedings. Two months ago a Negro was lynched at Lawrenceville, Judge Brand's home town, for alleged attack on a white woman. On that occasion Judge Brand also refused to ask for troops, although urged to do so, saying there was no danger. Two hours later the man was lynched.

Judge Brand admitted to a press representative, in an amazing interview, that he had realized the peril.

"While I want to discharge and have performed every duty which the law imposes upon me," he said, "I don't propose to be the engine of sacrificing any white man's life for all such Negro criminals in the country. Whatever other people

From "Along the Color Line," *The Crisis* magazine 2, no. 4 (August 1911): 142–143.

may think about it, I am in perfect accord with my conscience and my God. I would not imperil the life of one white man to save the lives of a hundred such Negroes. I am opposed to lynching, but if I had called the military and some young man among the soldiers was killed or some of the citizens of Walton County were killed I would never forgive myself."

DRAWING CONCLUSIONS:

1. Can you put Judge Brand's position in your own words?
2. What chance did a black accused criminal have for a fair trial in Judge Brand's courtroom?
3. If you were an African American living in Judge Brand's district, would you trust the criminal justice system?
4. What actions did the governor take?

5.2 THOMAS NELSON PAGE ON LYNCHING

Thomas Nelson Page was a popular author of stories and novels that painted a romantic view of southern slavery. As activists brought attention to the issue of lynching, many Americans, especially northern liberals, questioned whether more should be done to prevent lynching and punish mob members. Thomas Nelson Page represented white southerners who defended lynching and successfully argued that the nation should not intervene with the southern criminal justice system. This article was published in a mainstream, popular magazine by a man so well-connected that he was later appointed by President Wilson to be the ambassador to Italy.

GUIDING QUESTIONS:

1. What does Page say is the reason white southerners lynch African Americans?
2. What is Page's view of history?
3. What does Page think about progress?

Time was when the crime of assault [rape] was unknown throughout the South. During the whole period of slavery, it did not exist, nor did it exist to any considerable extent for some years after Emancipation. During the War, the men were away in the army, and the negroes were the loyal guardians of the women and children. On isolated plantations and in lonely neighborhoods, women were as secure as in the streets of Boston or New York.

Then came the period and process of Reconstruction, with its teachings. Among these was the teaching that the negro was the equal of the white, that the white was his enemy, and that he must assert his equality. The growth of the idea was a gradual one in the negro's mind. This was followed by a number of cases where members of the negro militia ravished white women; in some instances in the present of their families.

The result of the hostility between the Southern whites and Government at that time was to throw the former upon their own acts for their defence or revenge, with a consequent training in lawless punishment of acts which should have been punished by law. And here lynching had its evil origin.

It was suggested some time ago, in a thoughtful paper read by Professor Wilcox, that a condition something like this had its rise in France during the religious wars.

The first instance of rape, outside of these attacks by armed negroes, and of consequent lynching, that attracted the attention of the country was a case which occurred in Mississippi, where the teaching of equality and of violence found one of its most fruitful fields. A negro dragged a woman down into the woods and, tying her, kept her bound there a prisoner for several days, when he butchered her. He was caught and lynched.

With the presumption of local power by the whites came the temporary and partial ending of the crimes and assault and of lynching.

From Thomas Nelson Page, "The Lynching of Negroes—Its Cause and Its Prevention," *The North American Review* 178, no. 566 (January 1904): 36–37, 44–45.

As the old relation, which had survived even the strain of Reconstruction, dwindled with the passing of the old generation from the stage, and the "New Issue" with the new teaching took its place, the crime broke out again with renewed violence. The idea of equality began to percolate more extensively among the negroes. In evidence of it is the fact that since the assaults began again they have been chiefly directed against the plainer order of people, instances of attacks on women of the upper class, though not unknown, being of rare occurrence. . . .

From recent developments, it may be properly inferred that the absence of this crime during the period of Slavery was due more to the feeling among the negroes themselves than to any repressive measures on the part of the whites. The negro had the same animal instincts in Slavery that he exhibits now; the punishment that follows the crime now is as certain, as terrible, and as swift as it could have been then. So, to what is due the alarming increase of this terrible brutality?

To the writer it appears plain that it is due to two things: first, to racial antagonism and to the talk of social equality, from which it first sprang, that inflames the ignorant negro, who has grown up unregulated and undisciplined; and secondly, to the absence of a strong restraining public opinion among the negroes of any class, which alone can extirpate the crime. In the first place, the negro does not generally believe in the virtue of women. It is beyond his experience. He does not generally believe in the existence of actual assault. It is beyond his comprehension. In the next place, his passion, always his controlling force, is now, since the new teaching, for the white woman.

That there are many negroes who are law-abiding and whose influence is for good, no one who knows the worthy members of the race, those who represent the better element, will deny. But while there are, of course, notable exceptions, they are not often of the "New Issue," nor even generally among the prominent leaders: those who publish papers and control conventions.

As the crime of rape had its baleful origin in the teaching of equality and the placing of power in the ignorant negroes' hands, so its perpetration and increase have undoubtedly been due in large part to the same teaching. The intelligent negro may understand what social equality truly means; but to the ignorant and brutal young negro, it signifies but one thing: the opportunity to enjoy, equally with white men, the privilege of cohabiting with white women. This the whites of the South understand; and if it were understood abroad, it would serve to explain some things which have not been understood hitherto. It will explain, in part, the universal and furious hostility of the South to even the least suggestion of social equality.

DRAWING CONCLUSIONS:

1. According to Page, how is the history of rape connected to the history of slavery and emancipation?
2. How would Page's viewpoint influence readers' willingness to support African American access to education? Or civil rights, such as the vote?
3. What can you infer about Page's idea of progress? What to him would be progress for African Americans?

5.3 MARY CHURCH TERRELL REBUTS THOMAS NELSON PAGE

See 1.1 for an overview of Mary Church Terrell. In this document, she replies to Thomas Nelson Page's defense of lynching.

GUIDING QUESTIONS:

1. What did you think was the weakest part of Page's argument? How do you think Terrell will answer him?
2. What is Mary Church Terrell's explanation of lynching?

In the first place, it is a great mistake to suppose that rape is the real cause of lynching in the South. Beginning with the Ku Klux Klan, the negro has been constantly subjected to some form of organized violence ever since he became free. It is easy to prove that rape is simply the pretext and not the cause of lynching. Statistics show that, out of every hundred negroes who are lynched, from seventy-five to eight-five are not even accused of this crime, and many who are accused of it are innocent. And, yet, men who admit the accuracy of these figures gravely tell the country that lynching can never be suppressed, until negroes cease to commit a crime with which less than one-fourth of those murdered by mobs are charged. . . .

In the second place, it is a mistake to suppose that the negro's desire for social equality sustains any relation whatsoever to the crime of rape. According to the testimony of eye-witnesses, as well as the reports of Southern newspapers, the negroes who are known to have been guilty of assault have, as a rule, been ignorant, repulsive in appearance and as near the brute creation as it is possible for a human being to be. It is safe to assert that, among the negroes who have been guilty of ravishing white women, not one had been taught that he was the equal of white people or had ever heard of social equality. And if by chance he had heard of it, he had no clearer conception of its meaning than he had of the principle of the binomial theorem. In conversing with a large number of ignorant negroes, the writer has never found one who seemed to have any idea of what social equality means, or who expressed a desire to put this theory into practice when it was explained to him.

Negroes who have been educated in Northern institutions of learning with white men and women, and who for that reason might have learned the meaning of social equality and have acquired a taste for the same, neither assault white women nor commit other crimes, as a rule. . . Lynching is the aftermath of slavery. The white men who shoot negroes to death and flay them alive, and the white women who apply flaming torches to their oil-soaked bodies to-day, are the sons and daughters of women who had but little, if any, compassion on the race when it was enslaved. The men who lynch negroes to-day are, as a rule, the children of women who sat by their firesides happy and proud in the possession and affection

From Mary Church Terrell, "Lynching from a Negro's Point of View," *The North American Review* 178, no. 571 (June 1904), 853–854, 855–856, 861.

of their own children, while they looked with unpitying eye and adamantine heart upon the anguish of slave mothers whose children had been sold away, when not overtaken by a sadder fate.

DRAWING CONCLUSIONS:

1. How does Terrell counter the arguments of Page? What is her most convincing point?
2. To what extent does Terrell display an upper-class perspective?
3. Page did not discuss home life, but Terrell paints a portrait of a slaveholding family sitting by the fireside. What does this passage reveal about the importance of home life for Terrell? What does it say about how the immorality of slavery is passed down through generations?

5.4 THEODORE ROOSEVELT ON LYNCHING AND RAPE

Theodore Roosevelt became president when McKinley was assassinated in 1901, and then was elected on his own in 1904. Roosevelt championed Progressive causes and was willing to use the power of the federal government to curtail businesses excesses. For example, he created the Food and Drug Administration (FDA) to ensure the quality of our supply of food and medicine. He also created the national parks system to protect wilderness from destruction. He enjoyed support from African Americans initially in part because of his close relationship with Booker T. Washington. Famously, Roosevelt enraged southern segregationists by eating lunch with Washington. But his overall legacy on race is mixed. Here, Roosevelt speaks on the issue of lynching. Activists had long called for the president to speak out and, more important, use the power of the federal government to intervene in the southern criminal justice system.

GUIDING QUESTIONS:

1. What would you expect a president to say or do if mobs killed more than fifty citizens a year, every year?

Every colored man should realize that the worst enemy of his race is the negro criminal, and above all the negro criminal who commits the dreadful crime of rape; and it should be felt as in the highest degree an offense against the whole country, and against the colored race in particular, for a colored man to fail to help the officers of the law in hunting down with all possible earnestness and zeal every such infamous offender. Moreover, in my judgment, the crime of rape should always be punished with death, as is the case with murder; assault with intent to commit rape should be made a capital crime, at least in the discretion of the court; and provision should be made by which the punishment may follow immediately upon the heels of the offense; while the trial should be so conducted that the victim need not be wantonly shamed while giving testimony, and that the least possible publicity shall be given to the details.

The members of the white race on the other hand should understand that every lynching represents by just so much a loosening of the bands of civilization; that the spirit of lynching inevitably throws into prominent in the community all the foul and evil creatures who dwell therein. No man can take part in the torture of a human being without having his own moral nature permanently lowered. Every lynching means just so much moral deterioration in all the children who have any knowledge of it, and therefore just so much additional trouble for the next generation of Americans.

Let justice be both sure and swift; but let it be justice under the law, and not the wild and crooked savagery of a mob.

From Theodore Roosevelt, "Sixth Annual Message," December 3, 1906, https://millercenter.org/the-presidency/presidential-speeches/december-3-1906-sixth-annual-message

DRAWING CONCLUSIONS:

1. What does Roosevelt think is the cause of lynching? The solution?
2. What specific actions did Roosevelt suggest to address lynching?
3. If you were an African American in 1904 and heard this speech, would you support Roosevelt in his next bid for office?

5.5 JANE ADDAMS ON LYNCHING

Jane Addams grew up in Illinois and went to Rockford Seminary as part of a growing trend of wealthy women to become educated at the college level. However, despite the increased access to university classes, very few jobs existed for educated women. Jane Addams resolved this dilemma by creating her own career. She founded Hull House and used her training in sociology to work with immigrants in the poorest neighborhoods of Chicago. Widely respected for her dedication and compassion, Addams waded into the controversy of lynching.

GUIDING QUESTIONS:

1. What criticisms does Addams have of lynching?
2. What does Addams think is the cause of lynching?

Punishments of this sort [lynching] rise to unspeakable atrocities when the crimes of the so-called inferior class affect the property and persons of the superior; and when the situation is complicated by race animosity, as it is at present in the South, by the feeling of the former slave owner to his former slave, whom he is now bidden to regard as his fellow citizen, we have the worst possible situation for attempting this method of punishment. But, whether tried at its best or worst, this method has always failed, and—more than that—has reacted to the moral degradation of all concerned.

We would send this message to our fellow citizens of the South who are once more trying to suppress vice by violence: That the bestial in man, that which leads him to pillage and rape, can never be controlled by public cruelty and dramatic punishment, which too often cover fury and revenge. That violence is the most ineffectual method of dealing with crime, the most preposterous attempt to inculcate lessons of self-control. A community has a right to protect itself from the criminal, to restrain him, to segregate him from the rest of society. But when it attempts revenge, when it persuades itself that exhibitions of cruelty result in reform, it shows itself ignorant of all the teachings of history; it allows itself to be thrown back into the savage state of dealing with criminality.

It further runs a certain risk of brutalizing each spectator, of shaking his belief in law and order, of sowing seed for future violence. It is certainly doubtful whether these scenes could be enacted over and over again, save in a community in which the hardening drama of slavery had once been seen, in which the devastation of war had taken place; and we may be reasonably sure that the next generation of the South cannot escape the result of the lawlessness and violence which are now being indulged in.

DRAWING CONCLUSIONS:

1. Does Jane Addams think lynching is part of a progressive society?
2. What does Addams think is the cause of lynching?
3. What argument does Addams make against lynching?
4. Does Addams accept the white southern argument that lynching is a response to rape?

From Jane Addams, "Respect for Law," *The Independent* 53, no. 2718 (January 3, 1901), 28.

5.6 IDA B. WELLS RESPONDS TO JANE ADDAMS

Ida B. Wells was born enslaved in Mississippi and emancipated by the Civil War. Her parents died of an epidemic. Though still a teenager, Wells ambitiously took guardianship of her younger siblings and worked as a teacher. She later moved to Memphis and became a journalist. When her friend, Thomas Moss, was lynched by business competitors to increase their share of the grocery market, Wells began to study the phenomenon of lynching. Her investigative journalism conclusively proved that the standard excuse for lynching, that it was a reaction to black male rapists, was false. After publishing her findings, Wells became a leading champion of the anti-lynching movement. Here she responds to Jane Addams's writing.

GUIDING QUESTIONS:

1. What does Wells think of Addams generally?
2. What criticisms does Wells have of Addams's understanding of lynching?

It was eminently befitting that *The Independent*'s first number in the new century should contain a strong protest against lynching. The deepest dyed infamy of the nineteenth century was that which, in its supreme contempt for law, defied all constitutional guaranties of citizenship, and during the last fifteen years of the century put to death two thousand men, women and children, by shooting, hanging and burning alive. Well would it have been if every preacher in every pulpit in the land had made so earnest a plea as that which came from Miss Addams's forceful pen.

Appreciating the helpful influences of such a dispassionate and logical argument as that made by the writer referred to, I earnestly desire to say nothing to lessen the force of the appeal. At the same time an unfortunate presumption used as a basis for her argument works so serious, tho doubtless unintentional, an injury to the memory of thousands of victims of mob law, that it is only fair to call attention to this phase of the writer's plea. It is unspeakably infamous to put thousands of people to death without a trial by jury; it adds to that infamy to charge that these victims were moral monsters, when in fact, four-fifths of them were not so accused even by the fiends who murdered them.

Almost at the beginning of her discussion, the distinguished writer says: "Let us assume that the Southern citizens who take part in and abet the lynching of negroes honestly believe that that is the only successful method of dealing with a certain class of crime."

It is this assumption, this absolutely unwarrantable assumption, that vitiates every suggestion which it inspires Miss Addams to make. It is the same baseless assumption which influences ninety-nine out of every one hundred persons who discuss this question. Among many thousand editorial clippings I have received in the past five years, ninety-nine per cent discuss the question upon the presumption that lynchings are the desperate effort of the Southern people to protect their women from black monsters, and

From Ida B. Wells-Barnett, "Lynching and the Excuse for It," *The Independent* 53 (May 16, 1901), 31–32, https://digital.lib.niu.edu/islandora/object/niu-gildedage%3A24185

while the large majority condemn lynching, the condemnation is tempered with a plea for the lyncher—that human nature gives way under such awful provocation and that the mob, insane for the moment, must be pitied as well and fair minded people should so persistently shut their eyes to the facts in the discussion of what the civilized world now concedes to be America's national crime.

This almost universal tendency to accept as true the slander which the lynchers offer to civilization as an excuse for their crime might be explained if the true facts were difficult to obtain. But not the slightest difficulty intervenes. The Associated Press dispatches, the press clipping bureau, frequent book publications and the annual summary of a number of influential journals give the lynching record every year. This record, easily within the reach of every one who wants it, makes inexcusable the statement and cruelly unwarranted the assumption that negroes are lynched only because of their assaults upon womanhood.

DRAWING CONCLUSIONS:

1. Why do you think Wells begins with praise for Addams's Appeal? What does that tell you about how widely lynching was tolerated?
2. What specific argument and evidence does Wells use to counter the presumption that lynching was a response to rape?
3. When you believe something to be true, are you persuaded by someone arguing against you? How important is evidence in these situations?

5.7 TUSKEGEE PRESS RELEASE ON LYNCHINGS FOR 1914

Outspoken African American activists, such as W. E. B. Du Bois and Monroe Trotter, criticized Booker T. Washington, the conservative principal of Tuskegee Institute, for being overly cautious on the subject of lynching. Washington hired Monroe N. Work, the first black man to earn a master's degree from the renowned University of Chicago sociology department, to keep track of alumni. Work, with Washington's tacit approval, began collecting data on lynching. In 1913, Tuskegee Institute began sending out yearly press releases with data on lynchings from the previous year. Strategically, Work only drew on white newspapers for these statistics, insuring that he could not be accused of bias. Since Booker T. Washington and Tuskegee Institute were respected by white conservatives, north and south, prominent newspapers began running these press releases every year.

GUIDING QUESTIONS:

1. What do you think were the top accusations leveled against victims of lynching?
2. Which states do you think had the highest number of lynchings? The lowest?

THE LYNCHING RECORD FOR 1914

According to the records kept in the Department of Records and Research of the Tuskegee Institute that during the year that has just passed 52 persons were put to death by mobs. Of this number 49 were colored and 3 were white. The number of persons lynched in 1914 were apparently the same as for 1913 and is the smallest number for a year since the records of lynching have been kept.

Although the number of lynchings has not increased, there appears to be more of a tendency to lynch for any cause however trivial and to disregard sex. Of the 52 persons lynched in the past year only seven, two white and five colored, were charged with rape. Three of these lynched were women. One of these only seventeen years old for killing a man who it was reported had raped her. Another of the woman lynched were accused of beating a child to death, while the third woman and her husband were charged with setting fire to a barn. In the presence of their four year old child they were put to death.

The crime charged against persons killed were: murder, 13; robbery and murder, 6; robbery and attempted murder, 1; suspected of murder, 1; rape, 6; attempted rape, 1; killing an officer, 5; wounding officer, 1; murderous assault, 3; alleged murderous assault, 1; biting off a man's chin, 1; accused of wounding a person, 1; killing person in quarrel, 4; beating child to death, 1; trying to force way into woman's room, 1; stealing shoes, 1; stealing mules, 1; setting fire to barn, 2; assisting men to escape who had wounded another, 1; being founder under a house, 1.

Lynchings occurred during the year in fifteen states as follows: Alabama, 2; Arkansas, 1; Florida, 4; Georgia, 2; Louisiana, 12; Mississippi, 12; Missouri, 1; New Mexico, 1; North Dakota, 1; North Carolina, 1; Oklahoma, 3; Oregon, 1; South Carolina, 4; Tennessee, 1; Texas, 6.

From The Tuskegee Institute News Clippings File, 1899–1965, Lynching Files (1899–1966), Tuskegee, Alabama.

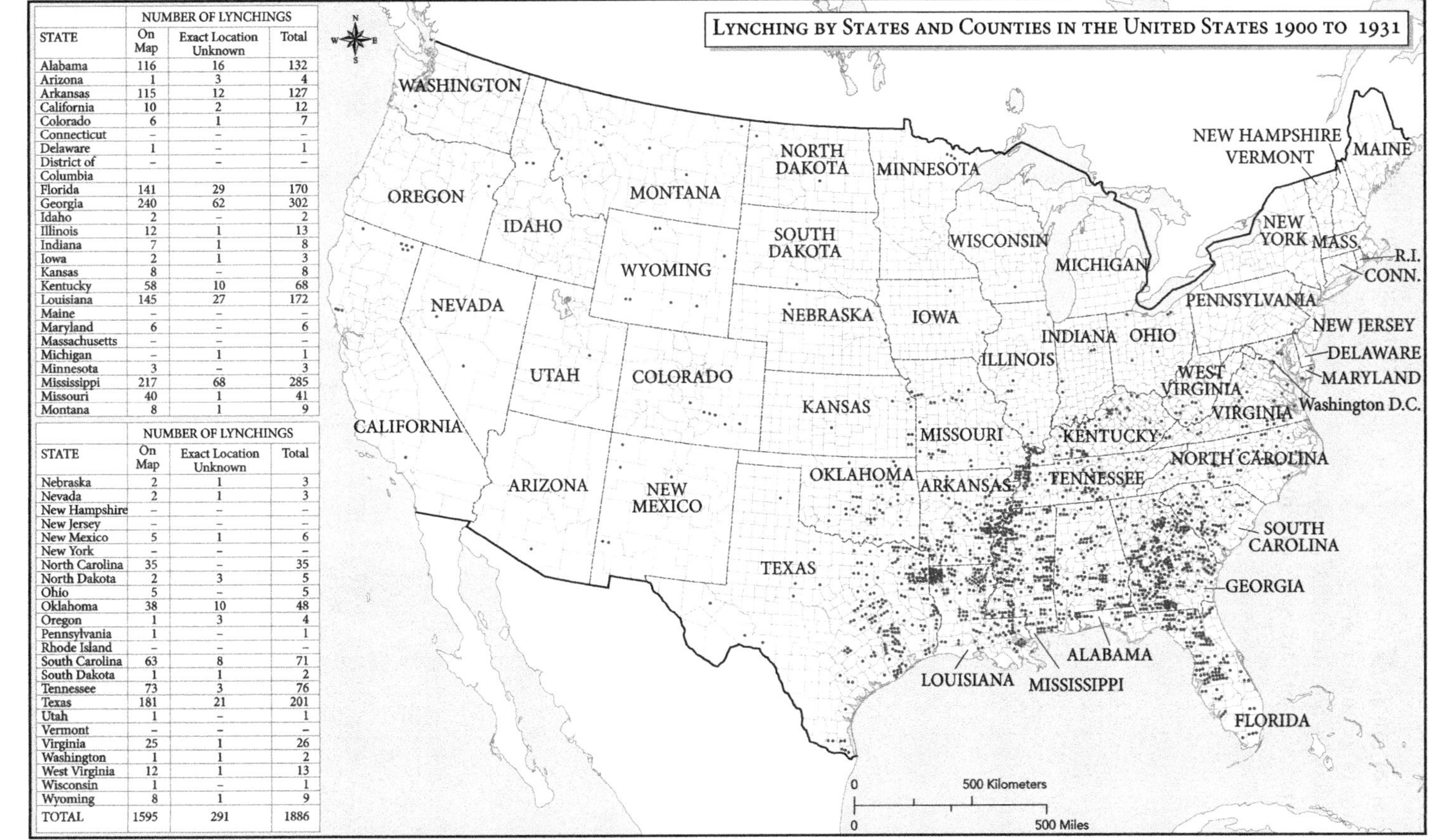

STATE	NUMBER OF LYNCHINGS On Map	Exact Location Unknown	Total
Alabama	116	16	132
Arizona	1	3	4
Arkansas	115	12	127
California	10	2	12
Colorado	6	1	7
Connecticut	–	–	–
Delaware	1	–	1
District of Columbia	–	–	–
Florida	141	29	170
Georgia	240	62	302
Idaho	2	–	2
Illinois	12	1	13
Indiana	7	1	8
Iowa	2	1	3
Kansas	8	–	8
Kentucky	58	10	68
Louisiana	145	27	172
Maine	–	–	–
Maryland	6	–	6
Massachusetts	–	–	–
Michigan	–	1	1
Minnesota	3	–	3
Mississippi	217	68	285
Missouri	40	1	41
Montana	8	1	9
Nebraska	2	1	3
Nevada	2	1	3
New Hampshire	–	–	–
New Jersey	–	–	–
New Mexico	5	1	6
New York	–	–	–
North Carolina	35	–	35
North Dakota	2	3	5
Ohio	5	–	5
Oklahoma	38	10	48
Oregon	1	3	4
Pennsylvania	1	–	1
Rhode Island	–	–	–
South Carolina	63	8	71
South Dakota	1	1	2
Tennessee	73	3	76
Texas	181	21	201
Utah	1	–	1
Vermont	–	–	–
Virginia	25	1	26
Washington	1	1	2
West Virginia	12	1	13
Wisconsin	1	–	1
Wyoming	8	1	9
TOTAL	1595	291	1886

MAP 4 TUSKEGEE LYNCHING

DRAWING CONCLUSIONS:

1. What is the tone of this press release? How is it calculated for the target audience?
2. White southerners who defended lynching argued that the practice was necessary to punish and deter black rapists. Does the list of accused crimes back up this argument?
3. Were you right in your projections of the best and worse southern states? Did anything about the state numbers surprise you?

POLITICS

During the late 19th and early 20th century, states of the former confederacy increasingly blocked African Americans from voting. Black citizens had less ability to support politicians who would represent their interests. See Document 2.9 from the section *Data on Black Life* for a table on African American representation in Congress. However, the African Americans who could still vote in the South and the increasing numbers that could vote in the North needed to decide which party to support. Since the Civil War, the majority of African Americans championed the Republican party of Abraham Lincoln, emancipation, and Reconstruction. But as time went on, the Republican party's commitment to black rights declined. Black citizens had to consider whether to continue to support the Republican party, shift their allegiance to the Democratic party, or try the new third party, the Progressive (or Bull Moose) party. Examine the following documents to evaluate the extent to which this was a progressive time of politics for African Americans.

GUIDING QUESTIONS:

1. What is the responsibility of the government to its citizens?
2. Are the rights of black citizens being protected at this time?

6.1 SPEECH OF SENATOR BENJAMIN R. TILLMAN, 1900

Benjamin Tillman represented South Carolina in the Democratic Party. Here he summarizes the history of how white southerners took away the vote from African American citizens. Without explicitly mentioning the violence, intimidation, and bloodshed of disfranchisement, he slyly alludes to such matters. The Fourteenth and Fifteenth Amendments were passed during Reconstruction and guaranteed the right to citizenship and the vote. During the 1890s these rights were systematically stripped by states of the former confederacy. Tillman and many other southern politicians drew on a specific version of history to justify segregation in the present.

We did not disfranchise the negroes until 1895. Then we had a constitutional convention convened which took the matter up calmly, deliberately, and avowedly with the purpose of disfranchising as many of them as we could under the fourteenth and fifteenth amendments. We adopted the educational qualification as the only means left to us, and the negro is as contented and as prosperous and as well protected in South Carolina to-day as in any State of the Union south of the Potomac. He is not meddling with politics, for he found that the more he meddled with them the worse off he got. As to his "rights"—I will not discuss them now. We of the South have never recognized the right of the negro to govern white men, and we never will. We have never believed him to be equal to the white man, and we will not submit to his gratifying his lust on our wives and daughters without lynching him. I would to God the last one of them was in Africa and that none of them had ever been brought to our shores. But I will not pursue the subject further.

From "Speech of Senator Benjamin R. Tillman, March 23, 1900," *Congressional Record*, 56th Congress, 1st Session, 3223–3224. Reprinted in Richard Purday, ed.,Document Sets for the South in U. S. History (Lexington, MA.: D.C. Heath and Company, 1991), 147. http://historymatters.gmu.edu/d/55/

6.2 REPUBLICAN PARTY PLATFORM, 1904

At the Republican convention in Chicago, representatives of the national party met to create their statement on what their party stood for. Some brought up concern over disfranchisement of black voters in the south. "Elective franchise" means the vote.

We favor such Congressional action as shall determine whether by special discrimination the elective franchise in any State has been unconstitutionally limited, and, if such is the case, we demand that representation in Congress and in the electoral college shall be proportionately reduced as directed by the Constitution of the United States.

From Republican Party Platforms, Republican Party Platform of 1904 Online by Gerhard Peters and John T. Woolley, The American Presidency Project https://www.presidency.ucsb.edu/node/273323

6.3 DEMOCRATIC PARTY PLATFORM, 1904

SECTIONAL AND RACE AGITATION

The race question has brought countless woes to this country. The calm wisdom of the American people should see to it that it brings no more.

To revive the dead and hateful race and sectional animosities in any part of our common country means confusion, distraction of business, and the reopening of wounds now happily healed. North, South, East and West have but recently stood together in line of battle from the walls of Pekin to the hills of Santiago, and as sharers of a common glory and a common destiny, we should share fraternally the common burdens.

We therefore deprecate and condemn the Bourbon-like selfish, and narrow spirit of the recent Republican Convention at Chicago which sought to kindle anew the embers of racial and sectional strife, and we appeal from it to the sober common sense and patriotic spirit of the American people.

From Democratic Party Platforms, 1904 Democratic Party Platform Online by Gerhard Peters and John T. Woolley, The American Presidency Project https://www.presidency.ucsb.edu/node/273196

6.4 ATTORNEY GENERAL LETTER TO PRESIDENT ROOSEVELT, JULY 5, 1904

Dear Mr. President,

I send you a copy of a speech which I made several years ago on the subject of disfranchisement in the Southern State. You will recall that the question arose whether if there was discussion of our reduction of representation plank it would be well for me at some time to refer to it. You will observe that my views are not in agreement with those of our platform. I do not think we for a moment can justify reducing representation on account of an unconstitutional denial of the right of suffrage.

. . . .

Very respectfully yours,
William H. Moody.

From Moody, William Henry. Letter to Theodore Roosevelt, July 5, 1904, Theodore Roosevelt Center at Dickinson State University, https://www.theodorerooseveltcenter.org/Research/Digital-Library/Record/ImageViewer?libID=o45923&imageNo=1

6.5 REVEREND MCPHERSON ON ROOSEVELT

Although southern states put barriers up for black citizens' right to vote, some African Americans managed to clear those hurdles to vote and serve as delegates to political conventions. Additionally African Americans could vote in northern states and constituted an important voting demographic. The majority of African Americans in the late nineteenth and early twentieth century voted Republican, the party of Lincoln and emancipation. Teddy Roosevelt in his 1904 presidential election enjoyed the support of many black voters. But by 1912 this support had waned. Progressives were impatient with the moderation of the Republicans and split off to form a third party, called the Progressive Party. This Progressive Party nominated Roosevelt as their presidential candidate. In this document a popular African American preacher argues that black voters should turn away from Roosevelt.

"The Fighting Parson," Rev. Dr. J. Gordon McPherson, known throughout the country as the militant black evangelist, whose fiery eloquence and forensic powers have thrilled thousands and won international fame as a speaker, reached the city Saturday evening and addressed three large gatherings Sunday at Damron Hall, in the interest of raising money for the New Hope Baptist church building. Dr. McPherson some weeks ago led one of the greatest evangelistic campaigns ever witnessed at San Diego. It was reported that thousands were held spell-bound and charmed by the matchless eloquence of the famed black preacher. Aside from the busy life of an evangelist, Dr. McPherson is editor of "the Voice of the West," the only illustrated Negro magazine in the far West.

As the doctor is a Spanish War veteran and leading Negro progressive, he has been a strong admirer of and has always championed the cause of Colonel Roosevelt.

In discussing the attitude of Colonel Roosevelt on the Negro question Sunday, Dr. McPherson said in part: "The once-strenuous 'Teddy' is playing the part of a weak-trimmer, who would do anything to win the election. He is smarting under his defeat at the Chicago convention, and the Southern Negro delegates remembered his ingratitude to the black soldiers who saved his life at Las Guasimas, when ambushed in Cuba. He repaid them by turning innocent men out of the army in disgrace because of the Brownsville riot.

The black delegates had a chance to even an old score and they did it with a vim. Even when thousands of Negro men and women had faith in Colonel Roosevelt, and blindly followed his leadership even into the new party, but his recent utterances place him in the front ranks of dangerous, self-seeking political demagogues, unworthy of a man that has been honored with the exalted position of the Presidency of this great nation. Ten millions of intelligent Negroes of America, with their billions of wealth, will not submit longer to political proscription, and Colonel Roosevelt and

From "Roosevelt Not a Friend of the Negro, Militant Black Evangelist Says T.R. Is Dangerous Demagogue," *Washington Bee* 33, no. 14 (September 7, 1912), 5. Accessed in America's Historical Newspapers, July 21, 2016, https://infoweb.newsbank.com/iw-search/we/HistArchive?p_action=search

his gang of visionary dreamers will realize that he cannot break the Democratic solid South by making the Negro voters of the South political scapegoats.

The platform of the Bull Moosers is not one of progressiveness, but of retrogression. My advice to the Negroes of this country who are dissatisfied with the grand old Republican party is to pin the Democratic Donkey ears back, grease him well and swallow Wilson, but by all means steer clear of the Bull Moose.

The once loyal Negro Progressives are deserting the so-called Progressive party like rats from a sinking ship, and since the spluttering Colonel has slammed the door of hope in the Negros face, we will do our best from now until the last ballot is cast to keep him out of the White House."

Dr. McPherson will go East in ten days as a delegate to the National encampment of the Spanish War Veterans at Atlantic City, N.J. and will deliver many addresses in the doubtful States against Roosevelt and the new party.

6.6 OSWALD GARRISON VILLARD ON FEDERAL SEGREGATION

In the antebellum period, the system of slavery organized all aspects of society, including the use of public space and appointments to political office. After emancipation, the collapse of slavery meant new possibilities. During Reconstruction, the presence of Union troops and the Freedmen's Bureau in the south meant all citizens could use public space, and that black men could vote and be elected and appointed to public office. But after the end of Reconstruction in the 1870s, white southerners embarked on a campaign to institute a new version of white supremacy that restricted public space and access to government positions with a new system of segregation. This innovation, although contested by African Americans, grew in states of the former Confederacy. Here Oswald Garrison Villard, a leading progressive (and descendent of the great abolitionist William Lloyd Garrison) describes the rise of segregation at the federal level after Woodrow Wilson became president.

Careful inquiry by a representative of the National Association for the Advancement of Colored People, and by newspaper men of the standing of Washington correspondents of the New York *Evening Post* and Boston *Advertiser*, has developed the fact that segregation of colored employees exists and is increasing, especially in the Bureau of Engraving and Printing, in the Post-Office Department, and in the office of the Auditor for the Post-Office, which is a part of the Treasury Department, and that is has begun in the Washington city post-office. As yet, segregation has not been introduced in the Treasury Building, where there are two hundred and seventy colored employees in the corridors and offices together with white clerks. It is defended by Mr. McAdoo as "an effort to remove causes of complaint and friction where white women have been forced unnecessarily to sit at desks with colored men." But there is no statement that there have been many such complaints or that they were head of under previous Administrations. Nor is it explained why colored clerks are taken out of rooms in which their sole companions are white men, or why, if there should be segregation because of the women, the Government does not segregate all its women clerks. Nor does Mr. McAdoo record the fact that in many instances the white clerks, without respect to sex, have gone to their colored associates and expressed their complete dissent from the Government's caste undertaking. He indignantly denies that poorer quarters have been given to the segregated, but eye-witnesses have told of colored women shut off in an unpleasant alcove in one office; of others quietly forced out of the lunch-room they had been using for nine years past and compelled to go into lavatories at the lunch-hour, of men clerks segregated behind lockers in one corner of a room in the dead-letter division of the Post-Office Department. Poorer accommodations for the segregated are the invariable law of segregation. The assignment of separate toilet-rooms to the races under threats of prompt punishment for failure to obey the rules has been another of

From Oswald Garrison Villard, "The President and the Segregation at Washington," *North American Review* 198, no. 697 (December 1913): 802–804.

the deeply humiliating features of the Washington segregation. To the colored workers all this segregating has been more brutal than a slap in the face. It is as if the great Government of the United States had gone out of its way to stamp them publicly as lepers, as physically and morally contagious and unfit for association with white people. Among them are perhaps veterans of Fort Wagner, of the Crater of Petersburg, and survivors of the triumphal march into Richmond of General Godfrey Weitzel's black brigade; certainly brothers and sisters of the black troopers who were good enough to die alongside of white men in saving the day at San Juan Hill are now learning to know the gratitude of Republics.

These colored people who are thus branded are not roustabouts, or corner loafers, or worthless laborers. They are educated men and women, college graduates many of them, from all over the country who have passed their civil-service examinations and entered the Government's employ with full faith in its justice, asking merely the right to serve on equal terms with their fellows. The readers of *The North American Review* will understand the bitter humiliation of the segregation orders if they can imagine themselves set apart as unworthy by brute authority, but they can hardly appreciate the added sense of injury which comes from the fact that this is an act of the Federal Government. The negroes have borne as patiently as the children of Israel bore their burdens, and wrongs of disfranchisement, the lynchings and burnings of innocent and guilty, the humiliation of the "Jim Crow" car, the constant personal insults of low whites; these were the acts of individuals or of States lately in rebellion. but that the Federal Government, under whose flag they have fought in every war, under whose aegis they are working, which struck their fetters from their limbs, should now take the side of the oppressors in the year of the fiftieth anniversary of Lincoln's Emancipation Proclamation—this is what hurts and rankles beyond all else. Is it any wonder the one of the leaders of the race of national renown writes that he has never seen his people so discouraged and so embittered as to-day?

DRAWING CONCLUSIONS:

1. Can you put in your own words what Tillman meant by saying "he is not meddling with politics, for he found the more he meddled with them the worse off he got"?
2. How does Tillman's view of black rights contrast with the vision of the Declaration of Independence that "all men are created equal" and the Constitution?
3. Can you put in your own words what the Republican and Democratic Party positions are on African American voting rights?
4. Analyze why McPherson wants black voters to reject the Progressive Party.
5. What arguments does Villard have against segregation? Do you agree that it is especially significant that the federal government is segregating?
6. Evaluate to what extent politics could be a pathway to progress for African Americans at this time.

TWO GIRLS IN 1900

The first image comes from a Stereoscope Company that made interesting pictures available to the public to view in 3D. From their description of this image, they wanted to show the viewers where cotton came from and possibly entertain them with an exotic view of a different kind of life. The vast majority of African Americans in the early twentieth century lived in the South (see Map 1) and worked in agricultural jobs. Children were often expected to work and contribute to the family economy.

The second image is of the daughter of an African American photographer in Atlanta, Georgia. Many of Thomas E. Askew's pictures were chosen by W. E. B. Du Bois to be in a collection he took to the Paris Exhibition of 1900 to showcase the black middle class.

GUIDING QUESTIONS:

1. Compare the dress, surroundings, and general context of each girl. What clues do you have about her class status?
2. How might each girl and her parents define progress? What goals might they have in common? What goals might be different? Please consider the categories of race, class, and gender in your response.

FIGURE 4 GATHERING COTTON ON A SOUTHERN PLANTATION, DALLAS, TEXAS

Source: Schomburg Center for Research in Black Culture, Photographs and Prints Division, The New York Public Library. "Gathering Cotton on a Southern Plantation, Dallas, Texas." The New York Public Library Digital Collections. 1900. http://digitalcollections.nypl.org/items/5e66b3e9-1793-d471-e040-e00a180654d7

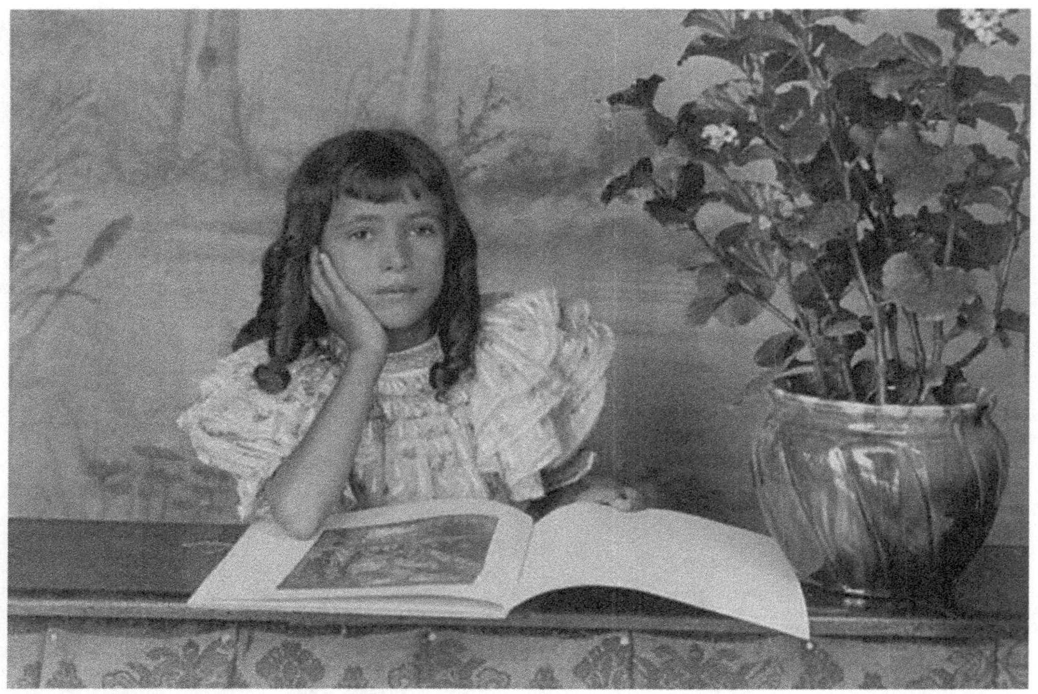

FIGURE 5 DAUGHTER OF THOMAS E. ASKEW

Source: Reproduction Number: LC-USZ6-2232. Library of Congress Prints and Photographs Division Washington, D.C. 20540 USA http://hdl.loc.gov/loc.pnp/pp.print

INDEX